PATRIOTIC PILGRIMAGE OF INDIA

"Many different types of monuments are raised in memory of Heroes. These memorials could be a road or building but the best monument of them all is a book which would pass on their memories to coming generations. I thank Rishi Raj for having built such a wonderful memorial that would last many centuries."

—**Colonel V.N. Thapar (Retd.),** (Defence Analyst & Father of Captain Vijayant Thapar, Martyr and Hero of Kargil)

"This book is a tribute to our freedom fighters and our brave soldiers which acts as an eye opener for the new generation as it is talks about our history and freedom struggle which the author exhibits through his travel experience."

—**Major H.P.S. Ahluwalia (Retd.)** (Renowned Mountaineer & Author), Arjun Awardee, Padma Shri & Padma Bhushan

---

"This book is a detailed and vivid account of the freedom struggle and wars fought by our brave men. The effort and energy that Rishiji has put in collating and describing the details are noteworthy. I truly recommend this book to all fellow patriots."

—**Brigadier Arvinder Singh (Retd.)**
(1965 & 1971 Indo-Pak wars veteran)

"Rishi Raj deserves to be congratulated for accomplishing such beautiful compilation of Martyrs deeds of valour and sacrifices in one book itself."

—**Mukesh Khetrapal**
(Brother of Second Lt. Arun Khetrapal, PVC, 1971 Indo-Pak war hero)

"I congratulate Rishi Rajji for writing this marvelous book and sincerely hope that present as well as future generations of our country would visit such sacred places of patriotism to realise true spirit of nationalism."

—**Yadvendra Singh** (Grandson of Shaheed-E-Azam Bhagat Singh)

"Indian forces are always prepared and more than capable to safe guard our mother land from any enemy. Bhagat Singh Rajguru, Sukhdev had sacrificed their lives at the very young age of 23 years. Every nook and corner of India is associated with great Sagas of such brave martyrs. This book pays rich tribute to these great sons of our motherland. I urge everyone to read this book."

—**Subedar Yogender Singh Yadav,** PVC

PATRIOTIC PILGRIMAGE OF INDIA

Rishi Raj

Published by
PRABHAT PRAKASHAN PVT. LTD.
4/19 Asaf Ali Road,
New Delhi-110 002 (INDIA)
e-mail: prabhatbooks@gmail.com

ISBN 978-93-5266-540-2
PATRIOTIC PILGRIMAGE OF INDIA
by Shri Rishi Raj

Translated
by Pt. Upendra Ram Krishna Shukla

Edition
2025

Price
₹ 500.00 (Rupees Five Hundred only)

Printed at
Shree Sai Printers, Sahibabad

Deadicated to Shaheed-e-Azam Sardar Bhagat Singh

Bharat ke liye tu hua balidaan Bhagat Singh
Tha tujhko mulk-o-kaum ka abhiman Bhagat Singh!!
Wah dard tere dil me watan ka sama gaya.
Jiske liye tu ho gaya kurbaan Bhagat Singh!!
Wah kaul tera aur dili arzoo teri.
Hai Hind ke har kuche me ailan Bhagat Singh!!
Pyara na ho kyo madre watan ke dulare.
Tha jaano-jigar aur meri shaan Bhagat Singh!!
Phansi par chadhkar tune jaha ko dikha dia.
Hum kyo na bane tere kadardaan Bhagat Singh!!
Har ek ne tujhe dekha hairat ki nazar se.
Har dil me tera ho gaya sthan Bhagat Singh!!
Bhulega qayamat me bhi hargeez na ae "Kishor".
Mata ko dia somp dilojan Bhagat Singh – Anonymous

FOREWORD

Even today, whenever I recall the memories of 5th July, 1999, I thank God for having selected me to accomplish this sacred mission of service towards my beloved nation and fellow human beings, thus, providing me an opportunity to find and fulfill meanings of my life. Intense war with Pakistan was going on that day and the Tiger Hill, our pride possession was still in the occupied control of Pakistan. After fighting for 22 days at Tololing with the enemy and unfurling our National Flag there after winning the battle, I was sent to Tiger Hill with my soldier companions. As a disciplined soldier of the Indian Army, I was thrilled and enthusiastic to undertake this mission and felt overtly anxious to regain the control of Tiger Hill. The time to exhibit such enthusiasm, valour, and bravery had finally arrived. At the height of 16,500 feet in shivering cold conditions that could have frozen blood, we set upon the task of climbing on to a very steep cliff-top. In this pursuit, six out of my seven companions fought bravely and became martyrs. I, the lone last man standing was also deeply wounded, had already taken three shots into my body, badly bruised and battered but the spirit of dedication and determination did not dampen even for a moment, hence didn't feel pain anywhere. I somehow managed to attack Pakistani soldiers by lobbying a grenade which killed four enemies. I am still unable to recollect from where I could garner such strength for accomplishing that feat but I can definitely say, at that time, I just had a solitary aim, motive, and passion of anyhow protecting the glory of my beloved nation – Bharat Mata.

My marriage date was fixed on 5th May, 1999 and I had reached Draas with my Unit 18 Grenadiers on 20th May, 1999. At the age of only 19 years, I not only got the opportunity to fight the war, but was also honoured with the highest gallantry award of our nation, the Param Veer Chakra – which was a historical moment of my life. That moment has added an entirely new dimension to my life. Every moment of this war is still etched afresh in my eyes. How our brave soldiers not only reclaimed every inch of our land from the deceiving neighbour, but also displayed to the world that however tiring may be the circumstances, in any tough challenging positions, the Indian Army is quite capable of protecting our country. When I was deeply wounded, same thoughts passed through my mind and I recollected that in the service of Bharat Desh, Bhagat Singh, Rajguru, and Sukhdev had sacrificed their lives at a young age of 23 years; in comparison, I had just shed a little blood. Our country, for centuries, has been the land of great warriors and in every war, India's warriors had protected the country even by making supreme sacrifices. In a way, I didn't exhibit anything unique but have just followed the high standards of morale and ideals set by those martyrs. Every place in India, however tiny it may be, has many stories of the sacrificing warriors. I am happy that Rishi Raj ji not only has visited those places personally to offer heartfelt tributes to the memories of those warriors or soldiers but has also made sincere endeavours to make others aware about the history of those places. The title of this book *"Patriotic Pilgrimage of India"* in itself suggests that this book will apprise us with the gallant stories of our committed warriors. This effort is not only unique but also is highly commendable, for which I congratulate Rishi Raj ji and sincerely hope that the younger generation of our country would go through this book so that they can know about the great wars of India, their history, the places associated with them and the great warriors. They should be able to appreciate the price paid for acquiring and maintaining Independence, the air of freedom which they breathe. Although we cannot repay the price by any means, yet at least be able to pay our homage, gratitude, and regards to the memories of those warriors. Thus, we can fulfill some of our responsibilities.

Rishi Raj ji has started the book spanning the period from the revolution of 1857 and justifiably ended it with the Kargil War. He has narrated deeds of valour displayed by Mangal Pandey, Bhagat Singh, Udham Singh, Ramprasad Bismil, Chandrashekhar Azad, Somnath Sharma, Shaitan Singh, Nirmaljeet Singh Saikhon, Arjan Singh, Sam Manekshaw, Manoj Kumar Pandey, Vikram Batra and numerous other warriors have been brought in this book altogether – making the book very useful.

I bow down to all the warriors, martyrs, their families and with these words, conclude and once again commend Rishi Raj ji for this book.

Karmaveer ko koi rok nahi sakta karm karne se
Kaun maar sakta hai use, jo darta na ho marne se

JAI HIND

Subedar Yogendra Singh Yadav
Param Veer Chakra

PREFACE

The history of our country stands witness to the fact that in pursuit of affirming our greatness, we had to struggle for centuries, or dare we say several eras. This struggle was not of a year or two but had lasted for about 600 years. First it was Moghuls and then English who ruled upon us. In our perpetual freedom struggle, thousands of well-known warriors have laid down their lives and the sacrifices of many unsung revolutionary freedom fighters have gone unnoticed. Their names, their sacrifices have been lost through the passage of time. In the struggle for freedom, every one of them contributed his or her mite by having made continuous efforts in their own distinct ways, following own views or doctrines. Although their ways and means might have been different yet their objective was the same – that was to attain independence and freedom. Approximately 7.5 lakh people have sacrificed their lives to achieve this objective without even caring for their families. Consequent to their struggle, the fortunate day arrived when we could see the Sun of Freedom set in at past midnight. After the independence, we were required to fight with those people too who were once a part of our nation. We shared the same legacy, language and fought together for the same objective. But, with the passage of time, when the circumstances changed – our objectives also changed and we were required to stand against each other. By this time, you must have recognised the nation referred to here. The last war with Pakistan was fought at Kargil. This war was one of the bigger examples of betrayal. Where, on the one hand, our Prime Minister was shaking hands to further cause of peace at Lahore, on the other hand, at the same time, Pakistan deceitfully took control on the hills of Kargil. It is quite unfathomable that despite having lost to India every time in the past, this country is not ready to learn her lessons. The greatest wound was inflicted by another country who by chanting *Bhai-Bhai* had stabbed us at our back. The agony of 55 years is still persisting in our country.

The struggle and strife, which began way back in the year 1857 at Barrackpore and Meerut and, subsequently, followed by the war of Kashmir in 1947, war with China in 1962, wars with Pakistan in 1965, 1971, and 1999, the common thing in all of them was that our valiant warriors have sacrificed everything they possessed including the supreme sacrifice of their lives without any grudge. Undoubtedly, they have done this with a solitary aim of safeguarding dignity and people of our country –nobody can have a slight doubt over this. The question arising here is that what have we given them in return. Whether we accorded them with the due respect which they richly deserved? Most of the times, we would get an answer, we have not been able to accord the due respect – which as a grateful nation should have been given to them. With the passage of time, as the new generations emerge one after another, we somehow tend to forget great deeds of these forgotten warriors. We should not let this go on. The only way forward to prevent this trend is to make our current as well as future generations aware about the gallant stories of warriors, freedom fighters, revolutionaries and also about the places related to them, inspire the younger lot to visit those places of supreme sacrifices for paying homage, respect, and gratitude. The objective of writing this book is an endeavour in this direction – to make today's generation fully aware about the architects of India who had made ultimate sacrifices for protection of our Motherland, thereby facilitating us to breathe in the free environment. I am of the firm view that every Indian is indebted to contributions of all such warriors, freedom fighters, revolutionaries whose debts cannot be repaid by any means, but we can lessen the debts by visiting those sacred places by meeting their families and also by spreading awareness these to younger generation.

I frankly don't have any qualms of being a historian or a great intellectual. I am only an ordinary man who nurses an aspiration to visit historical places of our illustrious country and in the pursuit, I have been fortunate enough to have visited many places associated with patriots where I could bow down in reverence to the martyrs – connecting them with historical perspective and importance. In this book, I have been able to provide details of about 50 such places associated with the martyrs and patriots. Therefore, readers are requested to share this book with all sections of society, especially with the children & young adults. I have sincerely tried to take reference from the available literature, Internet and concerned persons residing in these places for whatever information is provided in this book. In case any factual errors still remain, I express my apologies in advance.

I am confident and sincerely hope that you will like my efforts. I would consider myself successful in my endeavour, if only you draw inspiration to visit at least one place mentioned in this book and pay your homage to the martyrs.

–Rishi Raj

ACKNOWLEDGEMENTS

At the very outset, I pay my heartfelt gratitude for enabling me to write this book to my Ishta Dev Hanumanji, with my Guru Shirdi Sai Baba and Ma Saraswati who bestowed me enough intellect, strength, and capability to move ahead in my mission. My mother and father because of whom I exist in this world and only through their blessings, I am able to reach up to this level. My wife Sonia and loving children Niyati and Kartikeya – their love and cooperation provides me with new energy everyday. Without their support, undertaking so many travels might not have been possible. My late uncle Shri Jagan Nath Ji Chawla, from whom I got plenty of books in my childhood – expanded my educational level. My friends working in the Indian Army are my true mentors. The prominent amongst them are Padma Shree and Padma Vibhushan Major Haripal Singh Ahluwalia, Lt. General Pitamber Kishor Rampal, Ati Vishisht Seva Medal, Param Vishisht Seva Medal, Col. V.S. Thapar (father of Kargil martyr Capt. Vijayant Thapar), Lt. Col. Prabhu Raj, Lt. Col. Shashi Kant Sharma, Maj. S.P. Singh, Maj. Nooti Kumar Rathore, IG/BSF Shri K.S. Walia, Ex-Joint Commissioner of Delhi Police, Shri Mukund Upadhyay, Ex-Officer of BSF Shri Chauhan ji, Shri Chandra ji of Central Industrial Security Force.

The writing of book especially the extensive travelling all over India, would not have been possible without the kind support and help of my superiors, peers, and subordinates in my organisation. In this regard, my deep sense of gratitude goes with each one of them, starting with my senior Shri Sharat Sharma, who is a renowned photographer and an avid traveller himself. He has been a perpetual source of inspiration and guidance. The advice and kind cooperation extended by Shri Vikas Kumar have been very important in my pursuit as otherwise I could not have travelled so extensively. His maternal grandfather Late Malkhan Singh ji was a great freedom fighter from Aligarh, where a government hospital and a locality have been named after him. Shri Anuj Dayal, who hails from a proud soldiers' family. His father Late Maj. General Shri Narbadeshwar Dayal, Ati Vishishta Seva Medal was in the EME Branch of the Indian Army. He had played a pivotal role in procurement of advanced weapons to Indian Army. My colleagues Joby, Paramjeet Singh and Raksha Sharma, with whose support and cooperation, this book could be completed in time.

I express gratitude to Dr. Thinles, residing at Leh, who made my visit to that place memorable. My elder brother and sisters Smt. Savita Chawla, Shri Pradeep Raj, Smt. Ritu Harsh, and Smt. Kavita Bajaj – without their blessings, I could not have done anything. Special respect and gratitude is due for my elder brother Shri Naresh Gulati – who aroused cultural interest within me from the childhood. The cooperation of Shri Pradeep Chhabra, a friend of mine who has always shown a new way to me the entire VCRC fraternity.

My thanks to Sh. Ravi Kant Soni & Sh. U. K. Shukla for giving their valuable timing in editing of this book.

CONTENTS

1
FIRST FREEDOM STRUGGLE OF 1857

The rebellion of 1857 was the first national struggle for swadharma and Independence.

—Vinayak Damodar Savarkar

The very purpose of writing this book would have lost its importance for me without mentioning the first independence movement held in the year 1857. The name of Mangal Pandey is already written in the golden words in Indian History. The credit of launching first armed revolution against English Government goes to Mangal Pandey. He was born on 19th July, 1827 and he laid his life for the sake of his country at the young age of 29 years.

British had arrived in India in the year 1600 later they established East India Company. The objective of that Company then was to promote trade and business between India and England. Slowly, they started spreading their imperialistic designs. At the ports of Calcutta and Surat cities, godowns and offices were set up. After getting permission from Mughal Emperor Jahangir, trade started flourishing. The British during their stay in India could very quickly observe that Indian kings were a divided lot. Seeing the sorry state of affairs, the British understood that it was not very difficult to rule India and for achieving their sinister designs, they just needed to deploy single policy of "Divide and Rule". Then they started to work earnestly on this policy. First they tried to test this policy by making efforts in erstwhile Bengal State. In the meanwhile, by the year 1707, subsequent to the demise of mighty Aurangzeb, power of Mughal Sultanate had also started eroding fast. There had been no binding power which could have kept the country united and this weakness became strength for British.

Mangal Pandey

On 23rd June, 1757 at Palasi near Calcutta, a battle evoked between Bengal's Nawab Siraj-ud-doulah and the English force famously known as Palasi War. English force was led by Robert Clive. The anticipated fears then turned into a reality. The British conspired with three army chiefs of Nawab and one Seth (trader) to ensure that the entire force of Nawab could not turn up in full might for the battle and the Nawab ultimately lost the war. The name of Mir Zafar emerged as the biggest betrayer. East India Company's morale received great boost through this victory. In the year 1764, English Army also won the Buxar War and with this, an era of their dominance began in Bengal. Within the country itself, there were many selfish people with their vested interests – who could go to any extent just for furthering their own interests. Such betrayers became friends of the British. Those traitors often passed valuable tips about the shortcomings/weaknesses of their rulers to the British for personal

Statue of Mangal Pandey at Government Museum of Independence Movement in Meerut, Uttar Pradesh

gains and favours. History is witness to the fact that those evil betrayers contributed in dividing the country. With this fantastic initial success, the morale of the British shot up. Slowly, yet steadily, they expanded their area of operation with an ultimate desire to spread its control to entire India. From the business foray in the year 1757 to the year 1857, just within a century, merely a period of 100 years, the British could spread their empire over almost the entire India.

The hero of the armed rebellion in 1857 was Mangal Pandey, sepoy in 34th Bengal Native Infantry, who was posted at Barrackpore in Bengal. As a matter of fact, a new type of Enfield guns were issued to the soldiers on 29th March, 1857. The cartridges of these newly introduced guns were required to be opened by mouth. The cause for annoyance for the soldiers was that then it was believed that animal fat of cows and pigs was used for glistening them. This severely offended the sensibilities of Mangal Pandey, a Hindu Brahmin. He refused to carry out the orders to use this ammunition from his superior British officers. The fellow soldiers of the Army also supported the stand adopted by Mangal Pandey. In a way, this incident triggered the very first movement for Independence. Although the English historians term it as Sepoy Mutiny, yet as an Indian, I perceive it as a pure revolution, meant to be the first meaningful effort for attaining freedom (Independence). Veer Savarkar also recognises it as '*Swadharma and Swatantrata ke liye kiya gaya pratham rashtriya sangharsh*' (first national fight for attaining Independence).

On 29th March, 1857, Mangal Pandey took out his gun and gave clarion call to his fellow soldiers to come as that was the right time to finish those English fellows. Mother India was calling them all. He urges them to come and finish those *Firangees* (British). At that point of time, English Sargent Major Hewson came and ordered the troop to arrest Mangal Pandey. No soldier paid any heed to this order. Mangal Pandey shot at him and Hewson fell dead.

Thereafter, another English officer Lt. Bob came riding on a horse. Mangal Pandey aimed his gun towards Bob and fired, who fell down as the horse was hit by the bullet. Bob tried to shoot Mangal Pandey but with great speed, Bob was mutilated with sword by Mangal Pandey. Meanwhile, two other English armymen were killed by Mangal Pandey. By this time, Col. Wheeler came to the ground, but none of the soldiers was ready to touch Mangal Pandey. Mangal Pandey was also injured and blood was oozing out of his body. After some time, English soldiers went away from the site. Mangal Pandey once again exhorted his fellow soldiers to come forward to fight. But his exhortion could not elicit the desired impact from them, as some of them might have thought that the date of revolution (*bagawat*) would take place as originally scheduled on 31st May – and they didn't respond and others remained as mute spectators bound by the discipline of military force and, hence, didn't respond to the call of Mangal Pandey. Mangal Pandey at this stage shot himself as he never wanted to be held alive by the English Force. But, unfortunately, he survived and was taken to Sainik Hospital. He was later hanged till death on 8th April, 1857.

(Cellular Jail)

The place which stood witness to the first revolution is at Barrackpore, located 24 kms away from Kolkata. My dream turned into reality in July 2016 when I visited Barrackpore. In 2010, when a film on Mangal Pandey was released since then, his character had fascinated me immensely. Just after reaching Netaji Subhash Chandra Bose International Airport from Delhi, my heart was full of child-like anxiety to reach Barrackpore as early as possible. But the slow traffic reduced my travelling speed and yet could not dampen my enthusiasm. Just before a night of my visiting Barrackpore, to my delight, my friend Mahendra Niranjan had informed me that his brother was posted there as Major in Army. When I talked to his brother regarding my visiting plan, he told that the place where Mangal Pandey was hanged lies inside Police Academy, where entry of general public is not restricted. He also provided me with another vital information that even before Mangal Pandey, another sepoy, named Binda Tiwari was hanged there in the year 1824. The history of Binda Tiwari's heroic act repeated itself after 33 years. It might have been possible that somewhere in mind of Mangal Pandey, Binda Tiwari could have been occupying space as an idol. It is also not possible that there was no effort whatsoever for revolution before the year 1857. Definitely, there could have been small and sporadic efforts whose spark could not turn into full-fledged inferno and their efforts might have been crushed cruelly by the British. Another such incident I could get to know was during my visit to Vellore, Tamil Nadu in February 2016. When I saw the fort and verified history, some interesting facts emerged such as revolution was started in Vellore in 1806. It so happened that Two Infantry Regiments of British Army (Madras Army) were posted there. The soldiers were asked to replace *pagri* with hat, shave their beard and a badge made of cow's skin to be placed on hat – this had hurt their religious sentiments and soldiers reacted violently, resulting in death of 10 English officers and about 100 English soldiers. Although about 800 Indian soldiers who were involved in the revolution were shifted to different locations by the administration and revolt was crushed by the afternoon, British Government had been jolted by this rebellion. As a result, the then Governor Lord William Bentick was called back to England. Although Comdt. Col. Jilespi of Vellore could quell the struggle, yet this damage spread to three other areas. All such disputable ordinances were withdrawn and government declared that no work/ order provoking religious sentiments of soldiers will be done now.

Such a big incident and the first revolution remained unsung only in the pages of history and in place of it, the revolution of the year 1857 importantly hogged limelight and has pride of being first freedom struggle in realms of history. In this way, Mangal Pandey emerged as the biggest leader of the revolution. It can be seen that revolution in Vellore took place 51 years before the 1857 freedom movement. Apart from this, in the year 1824, Rani Kittur of Karnataka raised voice of dissent against British, thus preceding 1857 freedom movement by 33 years. It was necessary for me to visit Barrackpore after having seen the fort of Vellore.

Author Infront of Barrackpore Railway Station, Kolkata

I was welcomed by light drizzle on my arrival to Barrackpore. First thing I did at Barrackpore was to pay my regards and homage to Mangal Pandey at his memorial in Police Academy. This place is surrounded by big Banyan (*Bargad*) trees which stand as a mute witness to what had transpired that day. On the statue of Mangal Pandey, a noose (*Phansi Ka Phanda)* is shown as tied around his neck. I have never seen such a magnificent monument in the country.

Memorial of Binda Tiwari Ji at Barrackpore, Kolkata

A View of Mangal Pandey Garden at Barrackpore, Kolkata

After spending some time there, we went to the temple of Binda Tiwari. This is also located inside the Cantonment and general public is not allowed entry there. Temple has statues of Hanuman ji and Binda Tiwari who proudly dons military uniform. The tree on which Binda Tiwari was hanged is still there.

Little away on the banks of Hugli River within Mangal Pandey Garden, his statue is placed. There, I got an opportunity to talk to Lt. Col. Shashikant Sharma, a fellow Delhiite. He told me that Cantonment at Barrackpore was initially established by the British. This means that Barrackpore is the oldest Cantonment of India and probably is the only Cantonment where plots and houses have been given on lease to the civil population. After getting such interesting pieces of information from him, I proceeded towards Kolkata. Now, I will tell my readers about the impact of 1857 freedom movement on Delhi.

Similarly, on 10th May, 1857, first armed revolution at Meerut, Uttar Pradesh was carried out under the leadership of Dhansingh Gurjar. In his revolution, several people from many States in North India participated with immense zeal and great enthusiasm. English Government was shaken by these acts. As a matter of fact, new cartridges were issued to 90 soldiers on 6th May. As a token of rebellion, 85 soldiers out of 90 had refused to comply. English officers ordered to forfeit their weapons, strip them and put them behind bars. Subsequently, on 10th May, the revolution, under the leadership of Dhansingh Gurjar took place. All those imprisoned soldiers were helped to flee from the prison. Even these days 10th May is celebrated as Kranti Diwas.

Dhansingh Gurjar was later hanged to death at Meerut on a cross-road. This incident acted as a catalyst and incited other seekers of revolution and added fuel to the fire. That's why, it is believed that the revolution on a larger scale with wider participation had emerged from Meerut. After that phase, the rebellion gained pace and series of disobedience actions ensued. Thereafter, the prominent revolution arose, albeit a few in numbers had decided to unite together and plan a concerted fight against the tyrants. The most prominent amongst them were Nana Saheb, Tatya Tope, Rani Lakshmi Bai and her advisor Lakshman Rao, Kunwar Singh, Rao Tularam, Khan Bahadur Khan, Begum Hazrat Mahal, and Bahadur Shah Zafar. All these leaders had chosen 31st May for an all-out concerted rebellion and entire India was waiting for that day to arrive, but the destiny had something else in store. The small and sporadic incidents involving Mangal Pandey and Meerut had already alerted English Government. We could not succeed in realising our desire then.

Then, these prominent personalities had to retreat and had to start movement against British Rule in their respective areas. Bajirao II after having lost a battle against the British had shifted to Bithur, where he got a fort and many temples constructed. English Government paid him a pension of ₹ 8 lakh per annum in lieu of his Pune State. Since he had no son of his own, Nana Saheb was adopted. Till the time Bajirao was alive, pension was paid by the British Government but upon his death, the government refused to accept Nana Saheb as his successor. The pension was discontinued and, owing, to this, Nana Saheb also revolted against the British. In the town of Bithur, Tatya Tope, Nana Saheb, his elder brother

Tatya Tope

Rao Saheb and Rani Lakshmi Bai spent their childhood together. Under the guidance of Bajirao Peshwa, they were trained in horse-riding and sword-fencing and this training proved to be of immense use for Bharat Mata subsequently.

During my stay at Pune, I went to Shanivar Vada, which at one point of time was the official residence of Bajirao. Shanivar Vada was constructed in the year 1732 for Peshwa Bajirao, the Prime Minister of Chhatrapati Sahuji Maharaj.

Author at Shaniwar Wada

The total cost of this seven-storyed building was ₹ 16,110/- in those days. Up to the year 1818, till the time Britishers took away the reins of rule; this remained as the official residence of Peshwa Bajirao. After the year 1818, Bajirao shifted to Bithur in Uttar Pradesh. Shanivar Vada has got five doors for entry:

Delhi Darwaza
Narayan Darwaza
Mastani Darwaza
Ganesh Darwaza
Khidki Darwaza

Author at Bithoor Ghat on in the bank of Ganga

Bajirao who had a glorious history once in the past chose to reside at Mathura initially as per an agreement with Britishers and then later shifted to Bithur. Bithur also has its own prosperous religious history.

At one point of time, Kanpur (erstwhile Cawnpore) was inhabited by a large number of English population as many offices were located there. Nana Saheb and Tatya Tope challenged the sovereignty of British rule and had defeated them twice at Kanpur. But the two factors, lack of resources available with them and on the contrary, modern ammunition available with British kept on causing pressure on our freedom fighters. At Bareilly, for a short while, Khan Bahadur Khan defeated the British. Rani Lakshmi Bai of Jhansi displayed exemplary bravery to rattle the British. The history repeated here also when she had to leave Jhansi because of internal traitors and she was martyred on 18th June, 1858, going down fighting valiantly with British at Gwalior.

Rani Lakshmi Bai was born at Ganesh Wada, Assi Mohalla in Varanasi. After fierce fighting with British, she died at Gwalior – where her *Samadhi* is made. This place is not less than a pilgrimage for us. No woman fighter in India has got as illustrious place as occupied by Jhansi ki Rani in our history. As no Indian is unaware of Jhansi ki Rani – how

Author at Samadhi of jhansi Ki Rani Laxmi Bai in Gwalior

could I be? In August 2016, I along with my family had paid my homage and heartfelt respect by bowing to her *Samadhi*. I had the privilege of seeing her fort at Jhansi in February 2013. I felt blessed with this opportunity.

Tatya Tope was a great warrior. He was born at Yevla in Maharashtra. Up to his last breath, he fought valiantly for the Independence of our country. An Englishman named Parsikras had written that amongst all Indian revolutionaries, Tatya had sharpest mind. If few other revolutionaries had possessed similar abilities, India could have been freed from clutches of British. Along with Indians, even some Britishers were also amazed and influenced by his bravery.

Author with friends outside the fort of Jhansi

At Madhya Pradesh, in the village of Paron, Tatya Tope was betrayed. Mansingh, the *Jagirdar* of Narwar State of Gwalior, joined hands with Britishers – because of which Tatya Tope was arrested and was hanged on 18th April, 1859. When he was taken to be hanged, his last words were, "Today you can hang me, but in my place, thousands of revolutionaries will be born and your objective will not be fulfilled" (*Aaj aap mujhe phansi par latka sakte hain, parntu mere sthan par hazaro krantikaari utpanna honge aur aapka uddeshya kabhi bhi pura nahi hoga*).

In the revolution of 1857, following revolutionaries belonging to different places in India have participated:

1. Kanpur – Nana Saheb and Tatya Tope
2. Bareilly – Khan Bahadur Khan Rohila
3. Satara – Rangoji Bapu
4. Gorakhpur – Gajodhar Singh
5. Kullu – Rana Pratap Singh and Veer Singh

6. Jagdishpur (Bihar) – Kunwar Singh and Amar Singh
7. Sagar – Sheikh Ramjan
8. Faizabad – Maulavi Ahmedullah
9. Haryana – Rao Tularam
10. Sultanpur – Shaheed Hassan
11. Mathura – Devi Singh
12. Mandsaur – Shahzada Humayun
13. Raipur – Narayan Singh
14. Assam – Maniram Dutta
15. Allahabad – Liyaqat Ali
16. Sambalpur (Orissa) – Rajkumar Surendra Sahi and Ujjwal Sahi

The list cannot be exhaustive as numerous kings and kingdoms participated in the revolution whole-heartedly, whereas some other kings either remained neutral or had assisted British. We cannot even imagine discussing Indian history without mentioning these great martyrs. You can imagine the magnitude of revolt by just considering one fact that by the year 1857, British Government had sentenced deportment of 4,000 revolutionaries to Andaman & Nicobar for serving ignominious punishment known as *Kala Pani* those days. By resorting to such oppressive tactics, the British Government wanted to convey a message to public at large that anybody revolting against British Government will be dealt with very severely. But those passionate people who nursed a burning desire of working towards achieving Independence in their hearts and minds could not have kept quiet by any means.

Vasudev Balwant Phadke

Around the year 1870, another revolutionary rose in Pune to challenge the might of the British Rule – he was Vasudev Balwant Phadke. He was born on 4th November, 1845 at Raigad, Maharashtra. At the age of 15, he got a government job. On getting news about his mother's illness, he approached English Officer for leave request. Not only the leave was declined but he was racially abused and scolded for being Indian. Even then he had proceeded for his residence, on reaching home he found that mother had already passed away. He was terribly agonised by the tragic incident and turned deadly against the British Rule. He assembled native tribals (*Adivasis*) and formed a formidable militant group named "Romoshi". The Britishers were afraid of this group in the seven districts of Maharashtra.

One day Britishers could arrest him and send him to a jail located outside India. It is believed that he undertook hunger strike unto death there and finally breathed his last. A monument is constructed in his memory near Pune Railway Station. During my visit to Pune in June 2016, I got an opportunity to pray for him at the monument. In this gallant way, Vasudev Balwant Phadke gave memorable support to the Independence Movement and became an idol for revolutionaries.

In the year 1871, Namdhari Sikhs started agitation against British in Punjab. They were opposing opening of butcher houses at different locations by British and they initiated armed revolution, in which 66 Namdhari Sikhs became martyrs. This entire mission was pursued under the leadership of Satguru Ramsingh ji. This supreme sacrifice by Namdhari Sikhs can never be forgotten.

Satguru Ram Singh Ji

After some time, during the year 1897, acute plague epidemic broke out in Maharashtra. English Government had sent an English Officer Mr. Rand for taking

Chapekar Brothers

remedial measures. He grossly misbehaved with the residents of Pune by inflicting cruelty. Such gross misconduct pinched the conscious of three Maharashtrian brothers – Damodar, Balkrishna, and Vasudev Chapekar and then they decided to kill Mr. Rand. On the occasion of Shivaji Jayanti, Chapekar brothers also reiterated the vow taken for freeing India from the Britishers. After attending a party, Mr. Rand was on his way back to official residence on a horse carriage. Chapekar brothers attacked from behind and fired at Rand, who died there instantly. Very soon the Chapekar brothers were arrested and subsequently hanged one after another. Damodar Chapekar was hanged on 18th April, 1898, Balkrishna Chapekar was hanged on 8th May, 1899, and Vasudev Chapekar was hanged on 12th May, 1899. This may be the first and only incident of three real brothers sacrificing their life for country. Mother India (Bharat Mata) and its grateful people can never forget their sacrifices.

In the year 1907, British Government was celebrating 50th year of crushing first Independence Movement of 1857. This celebration took place not only in India but also in England. This uncalled-for celebration had irked many patriots in India and elsewhere. Now, I will tell you about what transpired at London in opposition to the celebration. In the same year, India's famous revolutionary Veer Savarkar had stayed at India House, owned by another patriot Shyamji Krishna

Shyamji Krishan Verma

Verma. During his stay there, every day and night untiringly, he mobilised and met many freedom seekers who were working for India's freedom. Veer Savarkar abhorred the very idea of British government making fun of our first freedom struggle. British Government even staged many plays depicting Nana Saheb, Tatya Tope, and Rani Lakshmi Bai in poor light and mocking their martyrdom. Indian revolutionaries celebrated Golden Jubilee of Indian Independence Movement at the India House. It was proved that the struggle of 1857 was not a mere act of rebellion but was a fullfledged freedom movement. It was decided to celebrate this day in a highly memorable way. Shining badges were especially prepared for this occasion and all the revolutionaries displayed them proudly on their chests during the agitation.

Now onwards, the efforts to achieve freedom for our nation intensified even outside of India on foreign offshore land. Shyamji Krishna Verma took the responsibility of mammoth task of uniting Indian revolutionaries in London. Shyamji Krishna Verma was born on 4th October, 1857 at Mandvi in Gujarat. He was the first Indian who was conferred with MA and Law degree from Oxford University. Then, he became Sanskrit professor at the university. As I have told earlier, he had established India House in London, where Veer Savarkar, Madanlal Dhingra, Madam Bhikaji Cama, etc. came together. In the year 1905, he started publishing monthly newspaper named *'The Indian Sociologist'*. Shyamji Verma died at Geneva in the year 1930. He had a very strong last wish that his earthly remains – the ashes may be transferred to India, after attaining Independence. In March 2016, while visiting Kutch – the place Mandvi was in my mind. Earlier, I had known Mandvi for its beautiful sea beach and sunset only. In the year 2014, when Narendra Modi ji became Prime Minister – many a time he had mentioned the name of Shyamji Krishna Verma. This had caused curiosity in us as to who was Shyamji Krishna Verma and his contribution. Upon research, it was revealed

Ashes Urn of Shyamji krishan Verma inside Kranti Tirth at Mandvi (Gujarat)

to us that Mandvi is the birthplace of Shyamji. We immediately decided to include the place in our itinerary. A little away from sea beach, Kranti Tirth depicts our glorious history. After spending about an hour and also having seen the replica of India House, we went for seeing sunset. Our present Prime Minister Shri Narendra Modi went to Geneva while he was the Chief Minister of Gujarat and brought ashes of Shyamji Krishna Verma to Mandvi. A museum (Kranti Tirth) at his birthplace has been raised. I got an opportunity to visit there in March 2016 and to pay my regards. Kranti Tirth is replica of India House. Ashes of Shyamji Krishna Verma and information about other revolutionaries are also placed there. Whenever you visit Mandvi, don't forget to pay your regards at Kranti Tirth.

During his stay at London, Veer Savarkar spent time in solitude mostly in the library, searching for details of 1857 Freedom Movement. He has realised very well that people would have to be made aware of efforts made in 1857 – to keep the cause alive – otherwise the sacrifices of Nana Saheb, Tatya Tope, Rani Lakshmi Bai might go in vain, thus weakening the fight for freedom, which should not be allowed to happen. He wrote a book which was banned by British Government before it could be published. But for our revolutionaries, it became as sacrosanct as the *Bhagwat Gita*. Every revolutionary was provided with this book for secret reading so that they can know and draw inspiration from the 1857 freedom struggle. The name of this book is *1857 Ka Swatranta Samar*. Nobody could have imagined that a book would scare the mighty British Empire. Somehow with great effort, the book was published in Holland and its copies were sent secretly to France and other countries. In 1910, Veer Savarkar was arrested, and was sent to Cellular Jail to serve a sentence. Full name of Veer Savarkar was Vinayak Damodar Savarkar. He was born on 28th May, 1883 at Bhagur, Nasik. In June 2016, I went to Nasik and had good fortune of paying my regards to Veer Savarkar there – a museum has been made at his birthplace.

Bhagur is located by the side of Devlali Cantonment. After travelling with my family for about half-an-hour from Nasik we reached Cantonment – the sacred place. Museum is divided into ground and first floors. Many old photographs of Veer Savarkar speak volumes about Savarkar's heroic deeds and efforts for achieving freedom.

Once I got an opportunity to visit Veer Savarkar's memorial at Shivaji Park, Mumbai. This memorial, spanned into 6650 sq. metres, was inaugurated by the then President Dr. Shankar Dayal Sharma. This memorial has also got a library, and children are trained for boxing, judo, shooting and many other games there. Inside, a model of cell no. 123 of Cellular Jail is also kept where Savarkar was imprisoned.

Sacrifices and efforts of revolutionaries started yielding desired results. For attaining India's freedom, revolutionaries started assembling at America and Canada in addition to London. In this chain of revolutionaries, two more names had also joined – Lala Hardayal and Sohan Singh Bhakhna. These two assisted Kartar Singh Sarabha, Abdul Barakatullah, Ras Behari Bose in creation of Gadar Party in the year 1913. In the year 1914, father of Bhagat Singh, Shri Kishan Singh gave a donation of ₹ 1,000/- to the party. Bhagat Singh was highly influenced by Kartar Singh Sarabha and treated him as an idol. He always kept Kartar Singh Sarabha's

Kartar Singh Sarabha- Role Model of Bhagat Singh

picture with him. Then, a very tragic incident followed in which 55 revolutionaries of Gadar Party were hanged by the British Government. The prominent name amongst those martyred was of Kartar Singh Sarabha who sacrificed his life at the age of 19 years. Several of his associates were sent to *Kala Pani*.

Just after the revolution that took place at Meerut on 10th May, rebel soldiers gave call for *"Dilli Chalo"* and all of them marched towards Delhi. All these soldiers reached Delhi on 11th May. They all crossed Yamuna River through a bridge made with the help of boats. Delhi those days didn't have cantonments like Meerut. Cantonment was located at Village Rajpur in the nearby outskirts. Presently, we have famous North Campus of Delhi University located there. At present also, you can find a road named Rajpur Road there. The families of British Force took refuge in Flag Staff Tower. These days too, Flag Staff Tower is situated in the Ridge Garden of Delhi University, telling its own history. We have a road named Flag Staff Marg there. The present Chief Minister of Delhi occupies a residence located on this road. On 11th May, after a fierce battle that had numerous causalties, soldiers could seize control of Delhi.

Flag Staff Tower Located at Ridge North Delhi

Author in front of Badli Ki Sarai, Delhi

Revolutionaries then declared Mughal King Bahadur Shah Zafar II as their leader. British mobilised all their forces by summoning troups from Ambala, Punjab, and Meerut. In Delhi, several tussles broke out between revolutionaries and the English force at different locations. On 8th June, at Badli Sarai in Delhi, a very fierce battle took place in which rebelling sepoys bravely fought, displaying exemplary courage and valour but ultimately lost to British due to better strategic and modern warfare tactics deployed by British.

In this battle, Major General Sir Hennery Bernard was especially brought by British from Karnal, Haryana as reinforcements of force stationed at Alipur led by Major Wilson. In the fierce fight that ensued, 300 rebellion sepoys and British were killed. Today also, we can see two buildings, located in front of each other, telling tales related to its gory history. At one point of time, there used to be an inn (Sarai) nowadays only two doors are left as the remains. Owing to this, the colony is presently named as Sarai Pipal Thala. This place is situated in North Delhi on G.T. Karnal Road – near Adarsh Nagar Metro Station. This is also called Mutiny Memorial.

I take this opportunity to inform my readers about a similar type of memorial, probably you might have passed by so many times, but definitely might not have paid much heed. That memorial is located near Pulbangash Metro Station near Bara Hindurao Hospital. The memorial is named as Ajeetgarh Memorial, which was erected in the year 1863 in the memory of English soldiers who were killed in 1857 revolution. Here you can find a stone inscribed with the number of killed officers and soldiers. The total casualties inscribed there were about 3,857. This means that British suffered huge casualty. This building made of red sandstone is 29.5 metres high and resembles a church.

A View Of Mutiny Memorial Ajeet Garh, Delhi

Ultimately, by 20th September, 1857, British could regain full control over Delhi. Bahadur Shah Zafar was arrested and sent to Rangoon on exile to serve a sentence. His predicament is described in a poetic couplet written by him:

"Dam dame me dam naahi ab Khair Maango jaan ki
Ae Zafar thandi hui shamsheer Hindustan ki
Gazio me boo rahegi jab talak iman ki
Tab talak chalegi tege Hindustan ki"

A plaque showing list of British Casualities suffered in 1857 Revolution at Delhi

Third-century structure known as Ashok Stambh erected near Ajeetgarh Memorial is also a place worth visiting. That *Stambh* of 10 metres height is made by having assembled five pieces. During the period of Ninth Mughal King Farukhshier (1713-19), it was broken in five pieces due to a blast. In the year 1867, the *Stambh* was reassembled by joining those five pieces.

At the time of 1857 revolution, Red Fort (Lal Quila), the centre of Delhi Sultanat witnessed many ups and downs. The last Mughal ruler, Bahadur Shah Zafar, who took over reins in 1857, strived very hard continuously to regain the lost glory but could never match the control achieved during the regime of Akbar, Jahangir or Shahjahan. Red Fort is one of the most important buildings in India's history.

Red Fort, New Delhi

When our country became independent, our national flag was hoisted for the first time on the ramparts of the fort on 15th August, 1947. That tradition of hoisting National Tricolour followed by ceremonious address to the nation by the Prime Minister continues uninterrupted even these days. National Tricolour fluttering proudly takes us back to the Indian History and also reminds us of the martyrs and their illustrious lives. Red Fort is a symbol of our freedom struggle and national pride.

Red Fort was built during the rule of Mughal Emperor Shahjehan. It is figured as World Heritage Site in the illustrious list released by UNESCO. Red Fort derives it name from the red sandstones used in its construction. Within its premises, we have four memorials built to showcase the glorious history, whose upkeep and maintenance is done by Archeological Survey of India. These memorials are:

1. Swatantrata Sangram Sangrahalaya
2. Swatantrata Senani Sangrahalaya
3. Bharatiya Yuddh Smarak Sangrahalaya
4. Mumtaz Mahal Sangrahalaya

All these museums (*Sangrahalayas*) help us to know about our past, displaying vital information through materials and pictures used in history. Weapons (arms and ammunitions) used during 1857 revolution have also been displayed here. We can access many words of information about life and times of Netaji Subhash Chandra Bose and INA through exhibits here. In the year 1945, INA activists were court marshalled at Red Fort. This incident is exhibited aptly here.

Red Fort has a very vast expanse divided into many portions known as Diwan-e-Aam (Hall for public audience), Diwan-e-Khas (Hall for private audience), Nakkarkhana, Moti Masjid, Mumtaz Mahal, and Rang Mahal, etc.

One of the major attractions is the light-and-sound show held everyday at twilight hours in the evening, showing the spectators glimpses of our history and legacy.

We have another piece of history associated with the first freedom struggle in 1857 the Nicholson Cemetery – where British soldiers who had died in the conflict were buried, located near present-day Kashmere Gate Metro Station. The cemetery is so named as it has grave of Brig. General Nicholson. Kashmere Gate area was the main hub for revolutionary activities.

Display of weapons used in 1857 uprising inside Museum at Red Fort, New Delhi

Delhi, particularly North Delhi, had become the centre of revolution. During that period, General William Hudson inflicted the maximum blood-shed. He shot three Mughal princes named Miza Mughal and Khijra Sultan – both sons of Bahadur Shah Zafar and Abu Bakar, a grandson of the emperor. These Mughal scions were killed at a location near Delhi Gate, in a building near Ferozshah Kotla Cricket Stadium. This place is now called Khuni Darwaza, which was known as Kabul Darwaza at one point of time.

In August 2016, I got an opportunity to pay my regards to the revolutionaries at a memorial during my visit to Meerut. This memorial is built at Kali Paltan Mandir (Aughranath Shiv Mandir). In addition to this, we can see Pakistani tanks captured by our Army at Meerut Cantt. There, one can see a museum dedicated to 1857 revolution and another museum constructed by UP Government that has a big statue of Mangal Pandey that reminds us of the warrior. Meerut is located at a distance of just 74 kms from Delhi and can be easily visited within a few hours.

Author at Aughad Nath Shiva temple in Meerut- the place where 1857 Revolution originated

Government Museum of Independence Movement at Meerut, Uttar Pradesh

Kranti Udyan- a garden established in Memory of Martyrs of the Great Revolution of 1857 at Meerut, Uttar Pradesh

Some people don't consider 1857 revolution as successful but no one can deny the fact that it laid a firm foundation for the future freedom struggles. Although, it started due to the hurt religious sentiments, those revolutionaries who laid their lives smilingly have become instrumental in providing great inspiration. Veer Savarkar was quite correct in calling this movement as the first attempt for attaining *Swadharma* and Independence.

□

2
HUSSAINIWALA

Sarfaroshi ki tamanna ab hamare dil me hai.
Dekhna hai jor kitna bajue qatil me hai!!
Hai liye hathiyaar dushman taak me baitha udhar.
Aur ham taiyar hain seena liye apna idhar!!
Khun se khelenge holi gar watan mushqeel me hai.
Sarfaroshi ki tammana ab hamare dil me hai!!

In the last 20 years, I have visited Firozpur twice. Last time my visit was in the year 2000. Those days, one of my friends, Daljeet was posted there in Railways. I still remember that we travelled the length and breadth of the entire Firozpur in only a few hours on his motorcycle.

In the intervening period, after the passage of 16 years, I had got married and the God had been benevolent enough to have bestowed me with two lovely children. My children have now grown to attain 13 and 10 years of age respectively. I thought that this is the right time to instil patriotism (*deshbhakti*) in them. That's why, I made a conscious decision to let them start exploring those sacred places associated with the patriots. Second reason for me to embark on this holy sojourn was to inspire the youth of generation X to also visit these modern-day pilgrimage centres of patriotism through this book and the third pressing reason was that my friend Lt. Col. Prabhu Raj was posted at Firozpur. When he rang me up last time, he advised me to plan my visit early or else he may get transferred very soon. The experience of visiting a military area in the company of an army officer is quite unmatched. All these factors combined together brought me to Firozpur.

I set out, with my lovely family, for a long drive in my car to Firozpur from Delhi very early in the morning in March, 2016. Firozpur is at a distance of about 430 km from Delhi. By about 9 o'clock, we had already passed Ludhiana. On the way we bowed at the altar of Baba Murad Shahji located at Nakodar and then reached Firozpur at 1.30 p.m.

Straightaway, we went to Army Guest House. I have always found Army Guest Houses to be very cosy and comfortable. I never had any problem with regard to lodging too.

Prabhu had already planned for boating in Sutlej River as first thing in the long programme ahead. At 4 o'clock, my family accompanied by my friend Prabhu had reached Hussainiwala Boating Club. From there, we set out on a course to explore Sutlej in an Indian Army boat. Water of the river was very clean and looked beautiful in green hue. I just wondered at that site as to how the river that had travelled 2,000 kms till there was so clean. Beas River merges with Sutlej into a confluence at a location called Harike in Kapurthala district, just a few kms before Firozpur. A thought passed my mind that maybe one day, the water of Yamuna River in Delhi would also turn clean like that of Sutlej.

I had the privilege of seeing the origin of Sutlej River at Rakshas Taal during my visit to Kailash Mansarovar in the year 2012. Rakshas Taal is located on the opposite bank of Mansarovar lake and it is believed that Ravana had worshipped God Shiva at that location for years, standing on only one foot. Hence, the place is named Rakshas Taal. It is also said that water of Taal had turned saline because of the penance (*tapasya*) by Ravana, but I could not verify this as true from any reliable source. The placc is quite picturesque, a scenic delight. Kailash Mansarovar is located in Tibet and,

A Breathtaking dusk View of the Satluj River

in addition to Sutlej, three other rivers originate from here – Sindhu, Karnali and Brahmaputra. I am fortunate enough to have seen Sindhu too during my visit to Leh in the year 2007. I prayed to the holy river and also performed *achaman*, a ritual of seeping water through palms by devout Hindus.

Whereas, Sutlej River enters India via Shipika La in Himachal Pradesh from the Tibetian side and forms a confluence at Kapurthala after merging with Beas River. Thereafter, Sutlej flows into Pakistan from Firozpur. After it reaches Pakistan, Chenab River also merges with Sutlej. Subsequently, it merges with Indus at Mithankot in Pakistan.

Remains of Old Hussainiwala Station

My friend Prabhu told me that Sutlej consists of small islands inhabited by people and Sutlej on its way enters with into India

Entrance gate of Hussainiwala Border

at some places, then wanders into Pakistan at some places before finally entering into Pakistan. Boating experience in Sutlej was extremely enjoyable. We could see tattered remains of a railway bridge where a railway track used to pass in the past. At one point of time, Sutlej used to flow by the side of the Hussainiwala Railway Station but it has since drifted its path slightly away from the station. While we were boating, I told about this history of Sutlej to Prabhu to his utter astonishment. The word 'Punjab' literally means a land of five rivers and these rivers referred to here are – Sutlej, Ravi, Beas, Chenab, and Jhelum. In modern-day state of Punjab, we just are left with only three of them – Sutlej, Ravi, and Beas. The half-burnt bodies of great martyrs Shaheed Bhagat Singh, Rajguru, and Sukhdev were thrown hastily into the same Sutlej.

After enjoying the boating in Sutlej, we went to Hussainiwala Border, which is situated at a distance about half-a-kilometre from Shahidee Smarak (Martyrs' Memorial). Shahidee Smarak is the same place where great martyrs Bhagat Singh, Rajguru, and Sukhdev were cremated.

Everyday a beautiful colour lowering ceremony is held at Hussainiwala Border, just like the famous beating retreat at Wagah Border. In this ceremony, soldiers from Indian BSF and Pakistan Rangers lower down their national flags in the evening. In comparison to Wagah Border, the boundary gate and parading soldiers from both the countries are quite closer to each other. As the programme started, the number of people started swelling rapidly and their enthusiasm also started soaring simultaneously. The sky was filled with roaring chants of "Pakistan Zindabad" from Pakistan side and "Inqlaab Jindabad" and "Bharat Mata Ki Jai" from Indian side. The atmosphere was emotionally surcharged with the feeling of patriotism. Waving of national flags all around created a great atmosphere. We at our Indian side of border have common enclosures, where ladies and gents spectators sit together, whereas on another side, Pakistani men and women sit in separate enclosures.

Every time the soldiers raise their feet quite high before stamping hard on the ground spectators greet them with cheers by giving thunderous applause, which must be encouraging them to try even harder. I along with my dear children Kartikaye and Niyati waved the Indian Tricolour continually and we also chanted "Bharat Mata Ki Jai". By doing these, I felt very nice and my mind experienced soothing and peaceful feelings. Actually, one can find a *dargah* of Baba Hussainiwala near the border, hence this place became popular as Hussainiwala.

Hussainiwala was an open border till the time war broke out in the year 1971 and trade and business activities were carried out without any restriction before the war. During those days of open border, more traffic and movements used to take place as compared to that of Wagah Border. Those days, Firozpur was a lively and glittering city. The city was a very prominent business centre then, and the prestigious train of erstwhile undivided India – Punjab Mail, connecting Peshawar and Bombay used to ply via Lahore, Firozpur, and Delhi. That train was started in 1912 with a view to bring British Officers alighting at Bombay to Peshawar.

Samadhi of Martyrs Bhagat Singh, Rajguru, Sukhdev ji at Hussainiwala Border

Now, we will move from this border post to the most important place in our itinerary Shaheedi Sthal – where Bhagat Singh, Rajguru, and Sukhdev were cremated.

Now a question may arise as to how the great martyrs Bhagat Singh, Rajguru, and Sukhdev were cremated here if they were hanged in Lahore Jail? We have a theory to support this fact. They were to be hanged on 24th March, 1931 as per the initial decision by the British Government, but due to an apprehension of widespread backlash and possible revolt, the great sons of Mother India were instead hanged at about 7.33 p.m. on 23rd March. When an English officer intimated Bhagat Singh that the time for hanging him has now arrived, at that moment, Bhagat Singh was reading a book penned by Lenin. He told the officer to wait to let one revolutionary meet another great revolutionary. Then just after a minute, he hurled the book in the air towards the roof and said nonchalantly – alright, let us move now.

While walking towards the gallows, they were joyously singing a patriotic song:

"Mera rang de basanti chola, mera rang de; mera rang de basanti chola! Mae rang de basanti chola."

It is said that after the hanging, fearing riots may flare up in retaliation of this ghastly act, the British had cut their bodies into pieces, put them in bags and had taken the earthly remains to Hussainiwala for cremation – where instead of *Ghee*, they used kerosene for burning the pyres. Seeing the smoke emanating, the villagers started coming to the place. British then threw the half-burnt bodies into Sutlej and fled away. But the local people could sense that something was amiss and understood the evil design of British and they not only recovered those remains from the river but also cremated them with full honour.

This sacred pilgrimage centre of patriotism was initially a part of Pakistan. Seeing the attached sentiments of Indians, Government of India had obtained it from them in exchange of 12 villages of Fazilka in the year 1961. In the year 1968, Shaheedi Smarak was constructed in memory of the glorious trio. During the 1971 war, Pakistan Army damaged this memorial and took away the statues of three revolutionaries. With the efforts of Giani Zail Singh, the then CM of Punjab, its lost glory was restored in the year 1973. Here, we have two more *samadhis* too. One of these *samadhis* is of Batukeshwar Dutt ji, who was an accomplice of Bhagat Singh who had accompanied him in the mission in which Bhagat Singh had thrown a bomb in Central Assembly Hall. He had a strong desire to be cremated there by the side of his beloved comrade. The

Samadhi of Martyr Batukeshwar Dutt at Hussainiwala Border

Mother of Shaheed-E-Azam Bhagat Singh, Punjab Mata Vidyawati ji

fifth *Samadhi* is of Late Vidyawati ji, mother of Bhagat Singh. She has been conferred with the title of "Punjab Mata". She had also desired that her last rites be performed near *Samadhi* of her great son.

It was in June 1975, when, as per her desire, her cremation was done at *Shaheedi Sthal*. Mata Vidyawati had not given birth to any ordinary child but to a great hero, who, although is not bodily present with us in this world today, yet his memories and fame would remain intact with every Indian till the time Sun, Moon, and stars exist. In his last meeting with his mother, Bhagat Singh had requested her not to come for collecting his body, but instead send Kulbeer (his younger brother) for the same purpose. Bhagat Singh laughed loudly after saying this and told her that if you come you would weep and the people will say, "See Bhagat Singh's mother is weeping." Such type of valiant mother and such type of even more wily lion-hearted son will never be seen again. On every *Shaheedi Diwas*, i.e. 23rd March, a fair (*Mela*) is organised at this place, when

Samadhi of Punjab Mata Vidyawati Ji at Hussainiwala Border

Abandoned Railway tracks of Old Hussainiwala Station

thousands of people assemble here to pay their regards to the revolutionaries. The first Prime Minister to have visited this place was Shri Rajiv Gandhi in the year 1985 and the present Prime Minister Shri Narendra Modi has visited here in the year 2015 and had paid his heartfelt tributes to the revolutionaries.

Ticket Office of Northern Railway at Hussainiwala

At the same Shaheedi Sthal, we can see the remains of Hussainiwala Railway Station, standing as mute witness of our golden history. Station Master's office, ticket counter and railway track all have been displayed here. When the original Punjab Mail used to pass through Hussainiwala in its full glory, there used to be delight on the faces of people. Those days, Firozpur Station used to be very crowded during the arrival of Punjab Mail. Police in large numbers used to be especially deployed at the station. After all, many British officers used to travel by this train. Since Independence, this station is away from the limelight and stands isolated and is the last station of Northern Railways. At a distance of about 1 km from Hussainiwala Station, near an Iron Bridge, we still have the remnants of tracks belonging to Northern Railway and as a mark of historical reminder, Firozpur division of Northern Railways operates a train between Firozpur and Hussainiwala for one entire day on the occasion of Baisakhi every year. Such type of example is rarely seen in the history of Indian Railways. On the side of Pakistan, the next

Terminal Point of Northern Railway near Hussainiwala station

station on this erstwhile line is "Ganda Singh Wala", which is now a part of "Kasoor" District of Pakistan. Here, I would like to inform my readers that "Kasoor" is named so with reference to Kush – son of Lord Rama and Lahore is named after his second son Lav.

It is very hard to find any Indian who might not have heard about the sacrifices made by Bhagat Singh, Rajguru, and Sukhdev. They are so well known because such great revolutionaries will never be born in India again. Bhagat Singh, who was hanged at the age of 23, was born in a village named Banga in Layalpur, Punjab, now located in Pakistan. He was brought up in a highly patriotic environment since childhood. His grandfather Arjun Singh ji and father Kishan Singh ji were associated with revolutionaries and had always craved for the country's freedom.

Bhagat Singh received initial education at Banga, only. Since childhood, Bhagat Singh was full of patriotism. He inherited this virtue from his grandfather Arjun Singh, father Kishan Singh and uncles Ajit Singh and Swarna Singh, who were participating in freedom struggle since so many years. Father of Bhagat Singh had provided monetary support to Lala Lajpat Rai and Gadar Party. Bhagat Singh came in contact of an active member from Gadar Party, Shri Kartar Singh Sarabha. He was so impressed with Sarabha that he always used to keep his photograph in his pocket and was treating him as his ideal. He used to follow all the instructions and advices of Sarabha.

Kartar Singh Sarabha was hanged at the young age of 19. His ideals were adopted by Bhagat Singh who solemnly took a vow to sacrifice his life for country's freedom. During his childhood days, while child Bhagat Singh was digging with his small tender hands in an agricultural farm, his father enquired as to what he was doing. He replied that he was sowing guns so that a great number grow as a crop which can be helpful to fight for freedom against British. Since childhood, he was extremely passionate to free Mother India from the clutches of British slavery.

On 13th April, 1919, gruesome massacre was committed at Jallianwala Bagh, where English officer General Dyer got innocent Indians killed. This grave massacre shook the entire country and also deeply influenced the mind of boy Bhagat Singh. Next day Bhagat Singh went to Amritsar from Lahore and brought soil stained with blood in a bottle and took a pledge unto himself to avenge this cowardly act with British and take revenge for such ghastly killing of innocent people. In 1920, when Gandhiji withdrew his Non-cooperation Movement, the young Bhagat Singh felt deep anguish in his heart because he had been watching this movement closely and had great hopes from Gandhiji. Dejected by this decision, he thought that very big and drastic steps would be needed to be planned and executed that can alarm the mighty and cruel British administration. He did not take admission in the famous Khalsa College of Lahore because the college administration was known to have been sympathisers and supporters of British Government. Instead he opted to obtain admisstion to DAV College of Lahore. There he came in contact of Sukhdev Thapar, who also liked him and had been aspiring for country's freedom. Bhagat Singh was very brilliant in studies. He had great interest in English, Urdu, and History subjects. Apart from this, he was also keen in co-curricular activities such as dramatics and singing. Through these plays, he was inciting patriotism in youngsters. In this pursuit, he went to Kanpur. He started writing articles for revolutionary writer and thinker Ganesh Shanker Vidyarthi's Hindi weekly magazine *Pratap*. Before this heresorted to selling of newspapers for existence. During this phase, he came in contact with other luninaries of freedom struggle, prominent among them were Chandrashekhar Azad, Ram Prasad Bismil, Batukeshwar Dutt, Manmanth Nath Gupta and Ashfaqullah Khan – all of them having allegience with Hindustan Republican Association. These meetings added another dimension, direction, and impetus in all spheres of his life and efforts for achieving independence.

The association had executed one big thing for acquiring funds for freedom struggle as well as weakening British Government by carrying out robbery of government's Treasure from a train at Kakori Railway Station. This was not a mere act of dacoity but was a glorious chapter of Indian Revolutionary Movement. The mission took place on 9th August, 1925. Kakori is a small station near Lucknow. Here in the second class compartment of 8 Down Passenger on that day, three young boys named Ashfaqullah Khan, Shacheendra Bukshi, and Rajendra Lahiri boarded. Other seven members of group – Ram Prasad Bismil, Keshav Chakraborty, Murari Lal, Banwari Lal, Manmanth Nath Gupta, and Chandrashekhar Azad had boarded in third class and as per plan ₹ 4,500 were looted from the government treasure. During this action, a passenger was killed by mistake. In the Kakori case, Roshan Singh, Ashfaqullah Khan, Ram Prasad Bismil, and Rajendra Lahiri were convicted and hanged until death by the British Government.

After association of Bhagat Singh with Hindustan Republic Association the diminishing light of freedom struggle became more prominent. In the year 1926, Bhagat Singh, Bhagwati Charan Bohra, and Yashpal, etc. had formed "Bharat Navjawan Sabha".

In the year 1928, when Simon Commission reached Lahore, it was vehemently opposed under the leadership of Lala Lajpat Rai. During the demonstration against the Simon Commission, British officers beat Lalaji, who suffered serious injuries. This lathicharge (cane baton assault) was ordered by a British officer named Scott. Injuries suffered by Lalaji were so serious that Lalaji breathed his last after 10 days. His death caused deep anguish and anger amongst people from all over India. Lala Lajpat Rai envisaged that the following lines be taught to every child in the country:

Mera majhaab hak parasti hai
Meri millat qoum parasti hai.
Meri ibadaat mulk parasti hai,
Meri adalat mera antahkaran hai.
Meri jaydaad meri kalam hai
Mera mandir mera dil hai aur
Meri umange sada jawan hai.

A Picture of Revolutionary Durga Bhabhi

For taking revenge of Lalaji's gruesome killing, Bhagat Singh along with Rajguru had shot and killed English officer J.P. Sanders on 17th December, 1928. As per the original plan, Police Suptd. Scott was to be killed but on that day and time, Sanders came out in place of Scott and was killed. Bhagat Singh was not satisfied with this. Anyway, the very roots of British Government had been shaken by this bold retaliation. Chandrashekhar Azad had extended great help to Bhagat Singh. During that time, Bhagat Singh was sent to Calcutta from Lahore with the help of Durga Bhabhi. As by that time, Bhagat Singh had got his hair-cut and Britishers were not familiar with his changed looks. Taking advantage of it, Bhagat Singh dressed up like an officer, accompanied by Durga Bhabhi and his son Shuchi as his family and Rajguru as his servant took the rail journey. This entire group boarded second class of Calcutta Mail on way to Calcutta. Durga Bhabhi was a strong lady married to a revolutionary named Durga Charan Vohra, thus fondly called 'Durga Bhabhi', had donated her entire life in service of the revolutionaries. Despite knowing fully well that travelling along with Bhagat Singh could be quite risky, she had volunteered to undertake the mission of shifting him from Lahore to Calcutta taking along her small child named "Suchi". Durga Devi's husband was also a great revolutionary who had died while testing a bomb.

A Picture of Bhagat Singh Wearing a Hat taken at Ramnath Studio, Kashmere Gate, Delhi

At Calcutta, Bhagat Singh had met Jatin Das. From him, Bhagat Singh took training about making of a bomb. Initially, Jatin Das was not inclined to help revolutionaries, but, later on, when Bhagat Singh persuaded him, he agreed and gave his life in service of Bharat Mata. He, at Lahore Jail with Bhagat Singh, undertook hunger strike for 63 days – in the course, he laid his life down for glory of Bharat Mata. During my visit to Kolkata, I saw a crossing named after Bhagat Singh and also had seen Jatin Das Park. When the body of Jatin Das was brought to Calcutta, Record 5,00,000 people had assembled for his cremation.

In the year 1929, Bhagat Singh took decision to hurl bomb in the Central Assembly and also to spread pamphlets. It was decided to carry out this herculean task on 8th April. Batukeshwar Dutt was selected to accompany Bhagat Singh on this mission. Shiv Sharma and Jaydev Kapoor arranged a house on rent in Kucha Sitaram, a locality in Chawri Bazar, Old Delhi. Bhagat Singh, wearing a nice hat, got himself photographed at Ramnath Studio in Kashmere gate area of Delhi, just two days before the mission with an aim that when his photograph would get published in newspapers after accomplishment of the mission, the people would be able to draw inspiration and would learn about his revolutionary views. It is pertinent to mention here that people at large considered the revolutionaries as a bunch of violent youths only, whereas the ground reality was that they were a group of highly motivated and educated self-respecting individuals, who were not afraid to even lay down their lives smilingly in fight for national freedom.

At last that red-letter day arrived when Bhagat Singh and Hindustan Republican Association succeeded in making deaf ears of British Government listen to their voice. After hurling bomb in the Central Assembly, they shouted "Inquilab Zindabad, down with imperialism" and then threw pamphlets and bravely courted arrest. All of a sudden, the country was abuzz with the talks of a brave young man wearing a hat who had challenged the might of British Empire. In fact, this bomb was thrown to prevent British from drafting anti-labour policies. When labourers working in the factories learnt about this, they started following Bhagat Singh. At that point of time, the national activists were divided into two factions based upon their approach to win freedom – Naram Dal (party of moderates) and Garam Dal (party of aggressive). On one hand, leaders of Naram Dal believed to adopt moderate non-violent means like protest marches, non-cooperation public demonstrations, etc. whereas, on the other hand, Garam Dal leaders, like Bal Gangadhar Tilak, Lala Lajpat Rai, Bipin Chandra Pal, Bhagat Singh, Chandrashekhar Azad, Rajguru, Sukhdev, and Bismil, etc. held the more aggressive approach to teach lessons to the British. In this approach, violence whenever required was to be used. Now the nation had two leaders – one the Mahatma Gandhi and another Bhagat Singh. Fair-complexioned youth, about 5 feet 10 inches tall had become icon for younger generation. Bhagat Singh

Famous Trio of Garam Dal - Lal, Bal and Pal

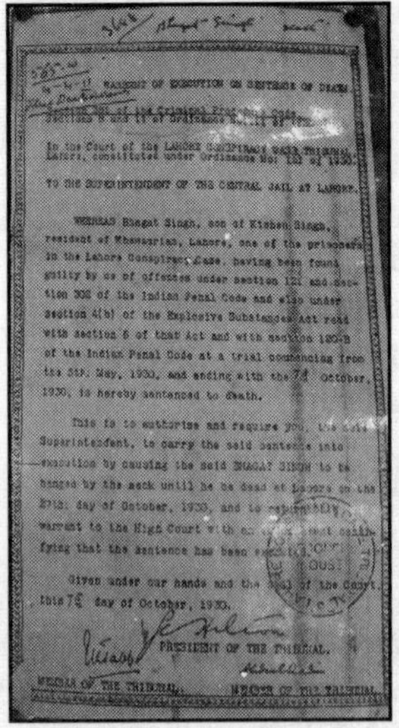

WARRANT OF EXECUTION ON SENTENCE OF DEATH

[illegible]

In the Court of the LAHORE CONSPIRACY CASE TRIBUNAL Lahore, constituted under Ordinance No: III of 1930.

TO THE SUPERINTENDENT OF THE CENTRAL JAIL AT LAHORE.

WHEREAS Bhagat Singh, son of Kishen Singh, resident of [illegible], Lahore, one of the prisoners in the Lahore Conspiracy Case, having been found guilty by us of offences under section 121 and section 302 of the Indian Penal Code and also under section 4(b) of the Explosive Substances Act read with section 6 of that Act and with section 120-B of the Indian Penal Code at a trial commencing from the 5th May, 1930, and ending with the 7th October, 1930, is hereby sentenced to death.

This is to authorise and require you, the said Superintendent, to carry the said sentence into execution by causing the said BHAGAT SINGH to be hanged by the neck until he be dead at Lahore on the 27th day of October, 1930, and to [illegible] warrant to the High Court with an [illegible] certifying that the sentence has been executed.

Given under our hands and the seal of the Court, this 7th day of October, 1930.

PRESIDENT OF THE TRIBUNAL.

MEMBER OF THE TRIBUNAL. MEMBER OF THE TRIBUNAL.

Death Warrant of Martyr Bhagat Singh

was not only fond of reading books but also possessed good knowledge of music, art, singing, etc. Ultimately, Bhagat Singh, Rajguru, and Sukhdev were pronounced guilty in Lahore conspiracy case and were sentenced to death by hanging.

In the jail, when Bhagat Singh was informed about this sentence, he recited the following *Doha* written by Kabir:

"Jis marne te jag dare mere maan anand,
Marne te hi paiye puran Paramanand"

It literally means "People (the world) are afraid of dying, the same death for my mind is a thing of joy, as only after dying, one can attain complete and abolute joy."

And then came the unfortunate day on 23rd March, 1931, when three of the greatest lion-like sons of Bharat Mata – Bhagat Singh, Rajguru, and Sukhdev were hanged.

What else can be a bigger sacrifice than smilingly greeting the death in service to the motherland at the age of 23 years. Kartar Singh Sarabha – the idol of Bhagat Singh, Khudiram Bose, Madanlal Dhingra and numerous other brave freedom fighters had made the supreme sacrifice of offering their lives and youth at the altar of Mother India. It goes beyond any doubt that whenever we talk about revolutionaries who worked for the freedom of India, the first name that strikes one's mind is that of Mother India. The following great lines of Bhagat Singh are still afresh and keep echoing in our ears:

"Mai khushi ke saath fansee ke takhte par chadkar duniya ko ye dikha dunga ki krantikari apne adarsho ke liye kitni veerta se baalidan de sakte hai!!"

"I would gladly accept to climb up on to the gallows, just to show this world that a revolutionary can bravely sacrifice one's life in pursuit of ones ideals")

Barki War Memorial at Firozpur, Punjab

After paying regards at Shaheedi Smarak, we went to the Barki War Memorial. There Pakistani tanks captured by our military heroes during 1965 war have been displayed. Even a milestone, brought by our troops that entered into enemy territory at Lahore in 1965 war, is also on display there. On the one hand, this memorial depicting bravery of Indian forces keeps Indians' head upward in pride and, on the other hand, we bow our heads in front of them to pay our respect and regards. Those heroes richly deserve the respect and regards from the indebted nation.

Entrance Gate to Shaheed Bhagat Singh's Ancestral House at Khatkar Kalan, Punjab

Prabhu arranged my night stay at the Army Guest House. Dinner was at his residence. Food prepared by Gayatri Bhabhi was excellent and particularly the pudding was very much liked by my daughter Niyati.

Well inside the courtyard of ancestral house of Shaheed Bhagat Singh

In the morning, after breakfast, we started for Bhagat Singh's ancestral house and Museum at Khatkad Kalan. Khatkad Kalan is known as

Shaheed Bhagat Singh Nagar. Bhagat Singh's house at Khatkad Kalan located on Chandigarh-Jallandhar National Highway is in no way less than a pilgrimage centre for us and being there to have *darshan* there was indeed a privilege. It was an emotional moment for me when I saw the bed, utensils, and almirah of Bhagat Singh. Within the house, there was a curtain behind which an earthen stove (*chulha*) is kept at a corner where the home-maker ladies used to prepare *rotis*. Just a kilometre away from this ancestral house, a museum is located, which is dedicated to Bhagat Singh, Rajguru, and Sukhdev, where many articles used by them – books, hand-written letters, newspapers full of blood, his horoscope, photographs of family members and revolutionaries, the pen by which the orders for hanging him were written, his ashes and few pieces of bone and many other articles are displayed. The Punjab Government decided in the year 2009

Flour Mill inside the ancestral house of Shaheed Bhagat Singh

Charpoy used by Bhagat Singh inside his ancestral house

Statue of Bhagat Singh at the entrance of Shaheed Bhagat singh Museum at Khatkar Kalan

News paper soiled by blood of Bhagat Singh, Sukhdev and Rajguru

to turn this museum into a world-class museum but the plan still remains in the pipeline. Need of the hour is to take up this matter at the earliest. I have written letters to Punjab and the Central Governments both for making this museum world class. This is not only a museum but is a pious place where the sacrifice of these heroes is evident in each and every molecule. After having seen these places, my respect for Bhagat Singh doubled and I took a vow that I would do everything possible to make younger generation aware about the lives and great deeds of these martyrs and also try to inspire them to follow these principles in their lives. If I can succeed in this pursuit, I would consider myself fortunate enough to have contributed my mite towards nation-building. Bhagat Singh often used to sing the following lines:

Few bones of the three revolutionaries Kept inside the Khatkar Kalan Museum

"Sewa desh dee jindariye badi aukhi
Galla karnia dher sukhalia ne.
Jina desh sewa vich pair paya
Ona lakh musibatan jhalia ne!!"

These lines mean that it is easy to talk about serving the nation, but walking the talk actually is very difficult.

Ashes Urn of Bhagat Singh, Rajguru & Sukhdev inside the Museum

Anybody who walks on the path of nation's service, needs to face lakhs (millions) of hardships.

I am fortunate that I also got an opportunity to go to Rajguru Nagar – the birthplace of Shaheed Rajguru – in June 2016. This place is about 44 kms away from Pune, Maharashtra. His place of birth has been converted into a small museum. Here the museum curator had shown us the place where weapons were kept hidden, the place of worship, and the secret door for going out to prevent detection by the British. Here, in a small container, soil from the memorials (*samadhis*) of all three martyrs is kept. A lamp remains continuously lit in front of the picture of Rajguru. Visiting this place was a highly gratifying experience for my soul. After having bowing down to the memories of Bhagat

Birth Place of Shaheed Rajguru Ji Located at Rajguru Nagar (Maharashtra)

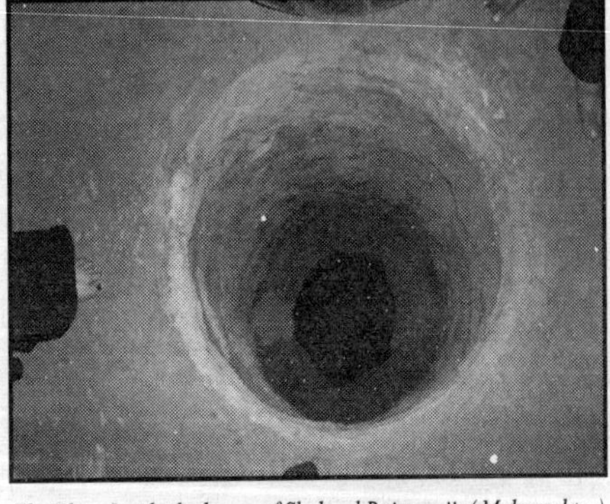

The Place Inside the house of Shaheed Rajguru ji (Maharashtra) where he used to hide his weapons

Another view of Birth Place of Shaheed Rajguru Ji Located at Rajguru Nagar

Singh and Rajguru at their respective houses, had I not visited the birthplace of Sukhdev Thapar, I wouldn't have satiated my mind. I, along with my companian Paramjeet, reached Chourah Bazar of Ludhiana in July 2016, where mostly people of Thapar Community reside. After paying respect to him at the place, my conscious was satisfied. After having visited these three pious places, associated with such great heroes, I felt as if I had been able to complete a great pilgrimage. In

Worship Place of Shaheed Rajguru Ji located at Rajguru Nagar

the fight to achieve freedom for the country, the name of Chandrashekhar Azad stands out as a bright star as bright as the famous pole star amongst the galaxy of freedom fighters. He was a great revolutionary.

A lamp lit eternaly in front of Rajguru's Picture

Soil from the Samadhi of Bhagat Singh, Sukhdev and Rajguru

Author at Birth Place of Sukhdev Thapar at Ludhiana (Punjab)

Many other people had joined freedom struggle inspired by his life full of valour and sacrifices. He was born to Shrimati Jagranidevi and Pandit Sitaram Tiwari at Bhawra in Madhya

Author at Chandrashekhar Park, Allahabad

Pradesh on 23rd July, 1906. His original name was Chandrashekhar Tiwari. At all the steps of his life since childhood days, he had offered tough resistance to the British Rule. In both the revolutionary missions of Sanders' assassination and Kakori case, he had played a prime role. I was fortunate enough for getting an opportunity to visit Alfred Park (present-day Azad Park) at Allahabad to pay my regards at his statue. Apart from this moment of personal gratitude, I also got an opportunity to visit Bhawra (Madhya Pradesh), the birthplace of Chandrashekhar Azad. We have a station named Dahod located on the Western Railway line connecting Delhi with Mumbai Central. It probably derives its name from the fact that it is on the boundary of two states, Madhya Pradesh and Gujarat, hence the name Dahod. Bhawra is located at a distance of 39 kms from Dahod. If you are on its visit, you can return to Delhi in a day. I consider myself to be very fortunate that I could visit both the places associated with Chandrashekhar Azad. The year in 2016, when our country was celebrating 70th anniversary of Independence. On this glorious occasion, Central Government had planned to organise special

Author at the birth place of Chandrashekhar Azad in Bhawra, Madhya Pradesh

A View of Neta Ji Bhawan Located at Kolkata

Author Inside the Neta Ji Bhawan, Kolkata

programmes at places related with martyrs, to show our gratitude and pay our respects to them. This plan was an initiative of present Prime Minister Shri Narendra Modi and had commenced by his visit to birthplace of Chandrashekhar Azad where he offered rich tributes to the martyr. Such type of initiatives will go a long way in inspiring the younger generation to visit such places.

Subhash Chandra Bose is another great name who took up the fight against India's misery for being slave nation and atrocities by British. Subhash Babu was born at Cuttack in Odisha on 23rd January, 1897.

During my stay at Kolkata, I made it a point to visit Netaji Bhawan – his residence. This has now been converted into a museum.

It was raised in the year 1909 by Shri Jankinath Bose, the father of Netaji. This museum is situated at Lala Lajpat Rai Marg (Sirani). In this historical house, one can see the office of Netaji, his bedroom, his dresses, and many old pictures on display. Here, we can get a glimpse of bright history of Netaji. The uniform which Netaji used to don in Azad Hind Fauj is also put on display in the museum. During my visit to Tokyo, Japan in June 2017 I to pay my homage by visiting at Renkoji temple built by people of Japan in loving memory of Subhash Babu. Japanese hold great respect for Netaji till today. Every year an his birthday i.e. 23rd January thousands of Japanese gather at Renkoji & hag their homage to Netaji. I also felt to be hounored visiting this place.

In the year 1941, Subhash Babu escaped to Berlin in a smart disguise outsmarting the British who had planned to put him under house arrest. At one point of time, Mahatma Gandhi and Jawaharlal Nehru had also visited this place. In the year 2007, the then Prime Minister of Japan also visited here and had paid regards. Col. Gurubaksha Singh a famous Sepoy of Azad Hind Fauj wrote a song "Netaji Ke Farmaan" – a few lines from the song are as follows:

"Utho soye Bharat ke nasibo ko jaga do
Azadi yu lete hai, Jawan le ke dikha do
Khunkhar bano sher mere Hindi sipaahi
Dushman ki safen tod do, ek tahalqa macha do
Azadi yu lete hai, jawan le ke dikha do."

□

3
KALA PANI : CELLULAR JAIL

"Mat Kaho Isko Kala Pani!
Tum suno yahan ki dharti ke
Kan-kan se gatha Balidaani"
– Ganesh Damodar Savarkar

In December 2012, we decided to undertake a visit to Andaman & Nicobar Islands, the place was once infamously known as *Kala Pani*. All of a sudden, this name *Kala Pani* started ringing in my ears. From the childhood days, we had been studying about *Kala Pani* and now that we were really going to visit the place, it had increased our curiosity manifold. This is one more sacred pilgrimage centre of patriotism where British mercilessly inflicted endless physical and mental torture to our Indian revolutionaries. Such was the level of cruelty that just by thinking of it would bring shivers down the spine of a common person. But all such cruelty was faced bravely by our revolutionaries as if they were being garlanded and finally they laid down their lives in service of Mother India and her independence. This is the same place which stood as a witness to the difficulties faced by our revolutionaries, which we cannot even dream of today. Because of such cruel treatment and offensive climate, Andaman was categorised as *Kala Pani*. British used this sentence as an equivalent to deporting any person out of country on exile to a place full of dire hardships. In this, the '*Kala*' word is taken from '*Kaal*', which means Death.

It was believed that anybody who goes there would never be able to come back alive.

Veer Savarkar had written – In today's world, there are many areas which geographically exist but have no history. Andaman Nicobar is one of such places. But this island has very deep-rooted and old relation with Indians. Because of its egg-like oval shape, it is named as Andaman.

Marco Polo had described Andaman as a vast island that has no ruler (king) of its own. The natives of the island were considered to be very cruel and were believed to be cannibals – Maneaters, who used to kill and eat people belonging to different tribe.

People avoided visiting these islands because of these gory and frightening tales till 17th as well as 18th centuries. Port Blair derives its name from Lt. Archibald Blair, a British national.

During Second World War, it was under the control of Japanese and in that period, Netaji Subhash Chandra Bose had visited here and called it 'Shaheed Dweep' or 'Swaraj Dweep' – a martyrs' island or Independence island. At present, we can reach here by sea route from any of the three Indian cities – Kolkata, Vishakhapatnam, and Chennai. There are total 572 islands in Andman & Nicobar. We decided to travel to Port Blair by Air. Flights are available from Delhi, Kolkata, Bhubaneswar, and Chennai. We took an Air India flight from Delhi to Chennai and took another flight from there to Veer Savarkar Airport of Port Blair. After taking off from Chennai, vast expanse of Bay of Bengal could be seen below for the entire duration of flying time till flight reaches Port Blair. The airport at Port Blair is named after the great revolutionary Veer Savarkar.

I could not resist my temptation to see Cellular Jail as soon as possible. Hence, we visited there on the very first day of our tour. This prison has stood as a silent witness to the cruelty inflicted on our freedom fighters by the British forces. This jail is known as *'Kala Pani'* because it is thousands of kilometers away from the mainland of country and is totally surrounded by water from all sides – nobody could have managed to flee from the prison and even if anyone succeded, somehow would not be able to escape the jaws of certain death. This jail

An Image Depicting atrocities against Indian freedom fighters inside the prison

was constructed to fulfill this evil thought. Inside the jail, Indian revolutionaries were subjected to immense torture. In the jail, *Kolhu* (a simple machine meant for extracting oil from seeds when rotated by bullock) was kept where the prisoners were used as manual force in place

An Image Showing the miserable situation of freedom fighters inside the prison

of bullocks. As a daily ritual, the freedom fighters were subjected to flogging and thrashing and were kept hungry as food was not provided to them.

In fact, just after 1857 revolution, British Government

Another View of Ross Island

Writer along with family at Ross island

had planned to isolate those voices of dissent by sending the revolutionaries to a secluded place, far away from Indian soil with nil proximity. Therefore, they had sentenced 4,000 such revolutionaries to an exile in Andaman and Nicobar Islands. Initially, the revolutionaries were sent to 'Ross Island'. There they were entrusted with the job of making residences for British officers by clearing and sweeping the forest. This island along with other islands was infested with many snakes and other dangerous animals. They were made to work throughout the day and after the tiring work were denied any rest or sleep in nights by the menace of swarms of mosquitoes. The actual number of revolutionaries who lost their lives by falling prey to the deadly malaria and other life-threatening diseases is not known. In the similar manner, 'Wiper island' was also prepared for the British officers.

English Government constituted a committee of two members for preparing a report on Prisoners' Exile at Andaman in the year 1890. The report submitted by them said that the exile was meant as a substitute of death penalty and the exile was not adequately punishing. Therefore, the report suggested keeping these revolutionaries in isolated cells to serve rigorous imprisonment for the first six months. The Cellular Jail came into existence to serve this ghastly purpose. The prison which was once infamous for the cruelty by the British has nowadays turned into a great monument that acts as a memorial for Indian Freedom Movement.

Work of constructing the prison had started in the year 1896 and was completed in the year 1906. Six hundred labourers and 3,00,000 bricks were used in its constrution. The middle minarate was kept as the centre-point of this prison and 693 cells were constructed around it in total seven galleries. It is constructed in such a manner that all these seven galleries end at one place, so that a strict vigil on the prisoners can be maintained at all times. Each cell had an area of 13.60 feet × 7.6 feet. These rooms were made in such a way that prisoners could never talk with each other. Forget about talking, they could not even see each other's faces. Every nook and corner of this prison stands as witness to brutality committed against our brave and fearless revolutionaries. How ironical it was, on the one hand, we had Swami Vivekananda professing about great cultural values and human ethos and freedom of expression at Chicago on 11th September, 1893, on the contrary, the British Government at the same time was busy in hatching sinister plans to oppress the freedom movement and finding various ways to inflict death and cruelty to Indian revolutionaries.

At the gate of Cellular Jail, there are two minarates on which 'Rashtriya Smarak' (National Memorial) is written, it was inaugurated by Morarji Desai, the then Prime Minister of India on 11th February, 1979. This is indeed an ideal monument to mirror our illustrious history.

While entering inside, one can see a museum built at the right side, which displays the life sketches of revolutionaries. First life sketch that you get to see is that of Baba Bhan Singh. He was brought here to serve a sentence in a case connected with Lahore Conspiracy. He was beaten so brutally that he could not survive and succumbed to his injuries. Thereafter, the life sketch of Mahavir Singh is depicted, who was the member of Hindustan Socialist Republican Association and a friend of Bhagat Singh. He participated in the hunger strike within the jail – in order to break his fast, jail staff had forcibly poured milk in his nose which resulted in his death. As a height of unmatched cruelty, jail staff threw his body

Entrance gate of Cellular Jail

into the sea. When this sad news reached the main land of our country, it caused a great resentment.

Similarly, we had another such great revolutionary named Indu Bhushan Roy. He was sent here to serve a sentence of 10 years' rigorous imprisonment in connection with Alipura Manik Kotala case. In the jail, inhuman and barbaric treatment was meted out to him which caused him to become mentally ill. Due to frequent tortures inflicted daily, he committed suicide by hanging on his coat tied with a grill. When you proceed a

Inner View of Cellular Jail

little ahead, you can see to your left-hand side an eternally lit lamp called "Swatantrata Jyoti" which continuously pays regards to the memory of those freedom fighters. When you walk further ahead, you can find a place that has many chairs arranged to watch a 'Light and Sound' show, describing the great heroic deeds of our freedom fighters at great length, conducted every evening. After passing through that place, you can see Hanging House on your right-hand side, where even today nooses have been kept hanging, to give viewers an idea as to how hanging used to take place. Whenever anybody was hanged, all other prisoners were ordered to see that act through their own eyes, so that they can know what is happening. After completion of hanging, lights on the top of minar used to be illuminated and the big bells were made to ring aloud.

Place meant for Last Bath Before execution

Interior view of Hanging Place inside the cellular Jail

In front of the Hanging House, one can see the *kolhu* placed, where, with the help of replica model, it is

Statues of revolutionaries extracting oil and making coconut fibres inside the cellular jail

displayed how prisoners were used in place of bullocks. Every prisoner was assigned with a fixed quota of work. Some of them had to extract oil through the *kolhu*, whereas others had to make threads out of coconut coir. Everyday, each prisoner was expected to extract at least 30-pound oil or else face severe beating. Drinking water was made available in very scant quantity. Veer Savarkar has detailed all such difficulties and hardships suffered by the inmates in his autobiography. He wrote that whatever may be the condition of prisoners, jail authorities had nothing to do with that. They only wanted 30-pound oil and, if not, they were subjected to severe scolding, abuses, cursing, and humiliation from Jailor Berry. He was considered to be one of the most cruel jailors. He had perpetrated serious cruelty and caused deep agonies to uncountable souls. Probably, because of this, his end was also very pathetic – he suffered with paralytic attack and had died in despair before he could reach his home in England.

While passing through those galleries, I had goosebumps all over my body due to the feeling of unabated devotion and respect towards those great souls. Deep inside my mind, I was bowing in gratitude again and again in front of them. I had to bow in front of them as our lives are indebted to them as without their sacrifice, I wouldn't have lived in the free environment and achieved success in my life. It is because of their sacrifices, we are able to lead a free life. The very moment I entered inside the cell of Veer Savarkar, I became highly emotional with the sense of pride and gratitude. I had heard many stories of his bravery and unmatched valour and had known how he had to undergo punishment of extracting oil from it and how his hands were tied with chains and made to hang upside down from the ceiling to prevent him from intercepting with fellow inmates. In that room, his picture has been placed with a garland over it. His intellectual brilliance is exhibited through the fact that he had written many great poems in praise of Mother India during his stay of 10 years in jail. He used to write those poems on the wall of his cell with the help of coal pieces and then memorise them. After his release from the prison, all those 6,000 lines so memorised were published in a book. His one famous sentence written in Sanskrit during his jail days is reproduced below:

"Aasindhu sindhu paryant yasya Bharat bhumika.
Pitrubhuhpunyabhushchhaivsa vai hindureeti smritah!!"

Meaning the only one who treats this Bharat Bhumi (Land of India) that is spread from Sindhu (in the north) to Sea (Sindhu in Sanskrit, located in the south) as its father land, sacred land is Hindu.

Savarkar always insisted on the use of chaste Hindi words in writings or conversations. He had translated many English or other language words into Hindi. He contributed several Hindi words, such as use of "Mahapaur" for Mayor, "Hutatma" for Shaheed, "Upmudreet" for proof, "Ekatva for monopoly, etc. Rajarshi Purushottam Das Tandon in an essay has written – *"Mujhe Sanskritnistha Hindi ke aandolan ki prerna Veer Savarkar se hi prapt hui thi!"* (I received inspiration to initiate a movement for promoting the use of chaste Sanskrit based Hindi from Veer Savarkar) Shri Ganesh Damodar Savarkar, brother of Veer Savarkar, was also imprisoned along with him in the same jail but irony of the destiny was such that both could not meet for two years. I could get another opportunity of paying my regards to Savarkar ji at a memorial built in front of Shivaji Park in Mumbai during one of my visits to the city in the month of June 2016.

Entrance gate of the Birth Place of Vinayak Damodar Sawarkar at Bhagur, Nasik.

Subsequently, I also got an opportunity to visit his birthplace at Bhagur, Nasik. I consider myself to be very fortunate for having the opportunities to visit all those places related to Veer Savarkar. I sincerely feel that every Indian shall try to visit such sacred pilgrimage centres of patriotism by taking out convenient time from one's busy schedule. We are in many ways indebted to them which we can never repay, but at least what we can do in their memory is to pay our homage and respect whenever possible.

Interior view of the Birth Place of Vinayak Damodar Sawarkar ji at Bhagur

Another Interior view of the Birth Place of Vinayak Damodar Sawarkar ji at Bhagur

Batukeshwar Dutt, another great revolutionary who had accompanied Bhagat Singh in hurling bomb in the Central Assembly on 8th April, 1929, was also sent to this jail. He was an active member of Hindustan Socialist

Republican Association. Some years after his release from jail, he had got married. Later on, he was infected by TB and had breathed his last during his treatment at AIIMS, Delhi. As per his desire, he was cremated at Hussainiwala, where his three friends – Bhagat Singh, Rajguru, and Sukhdev were also cremated. Even today, his Samadhi Sthal is present at Hussainiwala.

Names of some of the well-known warriors who were imprisoned in Cellular Jail are:

1. Veer Savarkar and his brother Ganesh Savarkar
2. Batukeshwar Dutt
3. Jaidev Kapoor
4. Motilal Verma
5. Baburam Hari
6. Pt. Parmanand
7. Ladha Ram
8. Indu Bhushan Roy
9. Prithvi Singh Azad
10. Diwan Singh
11. Pulin Das
12. Trilokinath Chakravarty
13. Gurumukh Singh
14. Yogendra Shukla
15. Maulana Ahmedullah
16. Nand Gopal Chopra
17. Bhai Parmanand
18. Mohan Singh
19. Upendra Nath Banerjee
20. Birendra Chandra Sen
21. Vishwanath Mathur

Apart from the above-mentioned greats, there were thousands of unsung revolutionaries who had happily laid their lives for Maa Bharti. Although mentioning their names may not be possible, yet nation cannot forget their supreme sacrifices made in service of Bharat Mata.

By the year 1937, with emerging of local governments and constant hunger strikes in the jails, control of British

Japanese bunker located at Ross Island

Government had broken down and by the onset of the year 1938, Cellular Jail was completely vacated. On 29th December, 1943, Netaji Subhash Chandra Bose had visited the place and paid his homage to martyrs with hoisting of National Tricolour. The area was in possession of Japanese during the intervening period from 1942 to 1945.

Mahateerth of Teerths, the Cellular Jail is such a pious place – which we should never forget and undermine its importance in our freedom struggle; rather, it is our duty to educate our coming generations about the revolutionaries and their heroic deeds – and, most importantly, not to allow the flame of patriotism get extinguished at any cost.

□

4
JALLIANWALA BAGH AND WAGAH BORDER

Kaum ke khadim ki hai jaagir Vande Mataram,
Mulk ke hai waste akseem Vande Mataram!
Zalimon ko hai udhar Bandook apni par garur,
Hai idhar ham bekson ka teer Vande Mataram!
Qatla kar hamko na qateel tu hamare khoon se,
Teg par ho jaega tahreer Vande Mataram!
Fikra kya Jallad ne gar qatla kar baandhi kamar
Rok dega jor se shamsheer Vande Mataram!
Zulm se gar kar dia khamosh mujhko dekhna,
Bol uthegi meri tasweer Vande Mataram!
Sarzamin England ki heel jaegi do roz me,
Gar dikhaegi kabhi taseer Vande Mataram!
Santari bhi muztreeb hai jab ki har jhankar se,
Bolti hai jail me zanzeer Vande Mataram

– Vishwanath Sharma

India's history will always remain incomplete if we don't mention the role of Jallianwala Bagh in it.

In the entire history of our Independence Movement, such a large and cruel massacre had not been carried out anywhere else by British Government. Neither India nor any Indian can ever forgive the British Government for such heinous and barbaric act. Although the British Government had been inflicting many serious wounds to Indians from time to time in the past, yet this was the most barbaric and

Author at the Entrance Gate of Jallianwala Bagh, Amritsar

gruesome attack on the innocent and innocuous gathering of unarmed people. Eyes of every Indian visiting this place becomes moist and tears start welling on seeing the ghastly reminders of cruelty left behind as bullet marks on the walls – we feel as if the marks are not the walls but are deeply imprinted in our hearts.

Jallianwala Bagh is situated in Amritsar, almost adjacent to the holy shrine of Harmandir Sahib in Golden Temple. Jallianwala Bagh is one of the greatest symbol of our freedom struggle and is the greatest pilgrimage centre for all the patriots. It is futile to have been born in sacred India and not having bowed in reverence at this place. My first visit to Jallianwala Bagh took place in the year 1995. That visit was definitely a very emotional moment. Right from childhood days, I had been reading and also listening to the stories of Jallianwala Bagh as to how General Dyer, a British officer, in a moment of unseen mental rage and hatred, had ordered to open fire on the innocent gathering of unarmed people, causing lot of bloodshed that filled the entire field with blood and mounds of dead bodies. Standing there, I was pondering about what was the fault of those innocent people? I was not able to fathom the mental bankruptcy of General Dyer. In fact, I was not much interested to think about the rationale or logic exercised by him as I am sure that no logical justification can be offered for this ghastly act of his.

ਗ਼ਦਰ ਦੀ ਗੂੰਜ

ਨੰ: ੩

Front Page of the newspaper Gadar-Di-Goonj

Before we try to understand Jallianwala massacre, we need to observe political scenarios and series of uprisings against the British Rule, which might have made the British so disparate and helpless that they had to resort to this ghastly act as the only way out.

Sikhs had very prominent role in that formation of Gadar Party in the year 1913. Lala Hardayal and Sohan Singh Bhakhna were perpetually making all-out efforts to intensify freedom movement in undivided Punjab. They had started publishing a newspaper in vernacular Punjabi language. In our Freedom Movement, Gadar Party played a very important part. In the year 1925, there came a time when 50 activists belonging to Gadar Party were sentenced to death en masse by hanging and many others were sent on exile to *Kala Pani*. Kartar Singh Sarabha was hanged at the young age of 19

Revolutionary Sohan Singh Bhakhna

years. He was the idol of young Bhagat Singh.

At one point of time, Bhagat Singh had met Sohan Singh Bhakhna at Amritsar. Bhakhna had been knowing Bhagat Singh as he was from a good and effluent family. He was also aware of Bhagat's revolutionary leanings. He asked "Bhagat, you do not have paucity of any materialistic objects. You are good-looking too, then why do you want to lead the tough life of a revolutionary?" Bhagat Singh replied to him, "For my aspiration to become a revolutionary, you, Gadar Party and Sarabha are equally responsible." Sohan Singh was amazed to hear this and asked, "How do you think so?" Bhagat Singh replied, "Patriotism, love, dedication, sacrifice, and the desire to do or die for the country has compelled me to become revolutionary. Now, I cannot stop". Sohan Singh, upon listening to this, was rendered speechless and hugged Bhagat Singh affectionately.

Upon hanging of almost all the Sikhs of Gadar Party and subsequent implementation of Rowlett Act, there was a deep sense of mass discontent in Punjab. On the other hand, despite constant efforts by British to divide people on the basis of religion, it could not dent the Hindu-Sikh-Muslim unity. Overall, Britishers' policy of 'divide and rule' was not getting the intended success here. Dr. Satyapal and Dr. Saifuddin Kitchlu were amongst the leading lights of unflinching Hindu-Muslim unity – which was annoying the Britishers. In the year 1919, during Ramnavami celebrations, people from both the communities took part with utmost zeal and brotherhood, which further annoyed the Britishers a great deal. Then, the enraged British got both Dr. Kitchlu and Satyapal arrested and sent them out of Amritsar secretly. This was not made known to

Dr. Satyapal

Dr. Saifuddin Kitchlew

the general public, which became the cause for great resentment because the general public had adored and respected them. A crowd of about 15,000 people gathered at a place and reached outside Dy. Commissioner's office for staging a, but when the procession reached on a bridge near railway station, British fired in the air to disperse the crowd but nobody was scared then. The force fired at the procession, killing 12 persons and also injuring 30 persons. This incident resulted in further escalation of public dissatisfaction and anguish. Due to such disturbance all around, a missionary school teacher Miss Sherwood had sent 600 children back to home on forced leave. On 11th April, when she was passing through Kucha Khurichan in Amritsar a few people had forced her to strip and beaten her. Britishers viewed this seriously and were quite alarmed by these turns of events. Now, they decided to plan terrible offensive in order to teach a lesson to Indians.

Lt. Governor named Michael O'dwyer is believed to have made this sinister plan of massacre of innocents in collusion with Colonel Reginald Dyer (on temporary charge of Brigadier General). He wanted to inflict a serious wound on the psyche of non-violent protestors and other people that could have taught a befitting lesson, however gruesome or cruel it could be with the motive to crush the now-assertive people of Punjab.

They had decided to carry out the barbaric act on 13th April, 1919. Sikh Sect was established on 13th April, 1699 by their 10th Guru Govind Singh ji. The day coincided with the celebration of Baisakhi, a famous religious and cultural festival of Punjab. Dyer could not have got a better opportunity than this to terrorise the people in an attempt to add insult to injury. Dyer for such heinous crime decided to use force (Army) for this. Flag March was done by Army in Amritsar City. They knew very well that a large number of people would assemble at Jallianwala Bagh for a peaceful meeting (*Sabha*). The meeting started at 4:30 in the evening and about an hour later, Dyer came to the place with his Royal Indian Army troupe. It was good that the passage to the entry gate was very narrow, thereby the armoured tank could not enter inside as was planned by him to cause maximum damage. He then ordered the troupe consisting of 90 Gorkha and 25 Baluchi Sepoys to take positions on the ramp and then ordered to open fire through their deadly 303 rifles on the hapless and unarmed gathering consisting of unsuspecting men, women, and young children. Dyer and his troupe had reportedly fired continuously for ten minutes and using 1,650 rounds almost till their ammunition exhausted. The unparalleled act of brutality and merciless massacre killed 388 persons and severely injured 200 persons as per the official figures. The unofficial reports suggested that more than a thousand people had died and two thousand had suffered injuries in the mad action of brutality and ugly display of power and authority.

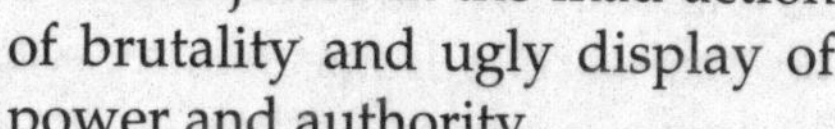

Sher-E-Punjab Sardar Udham Singh

The sudden and unexpected firing caused chaos all around the Bagh and ensued in stampede as people somehow tried to take cover or escape. Some people had died in the suffocating stampede too. Some people had jumped into a well in the garden to escape from the ongoing relentless firing. Later on, 120 dead bodies were taken out from the well. The bullet spots which are still visible on the wall wrench visitors' hearts with immense agony and anguish. This incident had stunned the whole of India and also Indian sympathisers living elsewhere abroad.

Next day, young Bhagat Singh, who was only 11 years old then, had gone to Jallianwala Bagh from Lahore and collected the soil drenched with the blood of martyrs. This incident had made a very serious impact on his life. Though lakhs of countrymen were anguished and felt perturbed by this brutal attack, yet one of them had been the most affected by the massacre, Sardar Udham Singh. At the time of this heinous killing, Udham Singh was present at the site, along with his friend, volunteering to serve water to the gathering. During his childhood, Sardar Udham Singh was called Sher Singh. His mother had passed away in the year 1901 and his father died later in 1907. His father was employed as gatekeeper in Railways. Udham Singh was born on 26th December, 1899 at Sangrur, Punjab and his parents had died early when he still was a young child. He was brought up at orphanage at Putalighar, Amritsar. He received his education there. Because he was an eyewitness to such ghastly crime, the scenes of the incident haunted his mind every day and night. He took a vow to avenge the massacre of innocents, he would definitely assassinate O' dwyer one day and thus would help in wiping off the blot on Punjab and Hindustan. He made this as the only aim in his life. After Jallianwala massacre, he had left the orphanage and started contributing in service to the country along with the other revolutionaries. Udham Singh was a staunch supporter of *Qaumi Ekta* (national integration), hence he renamed himself as 'Ram Mohammad Singh Azad'.

When he went to America in the year 1924, he came in contact with members of Gadar Party and on the advice of Bhagat Singh, he had brought 25 revolutionaries along with many weapons from there with an aim to intensify the freedom movement. By some means, British came to know about this development and they arrested him under

Arms Act. After some years, upon his release from prison in the year 1934, he reached London. There he set himself up for achieving his long-cherished aim of fulfilling his vow of assassinating Michael O'Dwyer, the Lt. Governor responsible for the massacre at Jallianwala Bagh. In the pursuit, he purchased a pistol and six cartridges and kept waiting for an appropriate moment. Lastly, that moment to avenge the ghastly massacre, for which he had waited for very long 21 years arrived on 13th March, 1940. On the day, while O'Dwyer entered in the Coxton Hall of Royal Central Asian Society, Udham Singh took out his pistol that was hidden in a book, and fired two shots at the planner of one of the most heinous massacres and extracted revenge for hundreds of innocent Indians. On the land of British, he could manage to assassinate a highly ranked British officer, thus proving that Indian revolutionaries didn't lack in patriotism. This incident stunned the mighty British Government. The valiant son of Mother India was hanged later in a London jail on 31st July, 1940. In his memory, a district is named as Udham Singh Nagar in the state of Uttarakhand, India. With the effort undertaken by the then MLA of Punjab, Shri Sandhu Singh ji, ashes of the martyr was brought from London and ceremonious cremation was done at Sangrur – his native place.

After having visited almost all the regions and States, it is my personal opinion that there is no other city like Amritsar in the entire India. The city is unique as it has all the charms of having rich cultural heritage, diverse enriched art, colourful dresses and palatable food. In these fields, before the partition in the year 1947, two cities were considered as advanced in Punjab. The first one in the list was Lahore and the second one was Amritsar. Because of their rich cultural and political heritage, Muslim League insisted for inclusion of Amritsar into Pakistan, whereas the Congress wanted to have Lahore in India. Both these wonderful cities are located nearby. Distance of Amritsar from Lahore is only 49.5 kms. Lahore was inhabited by not only Hindus and Punjabis, but also had large population of Bengalis and Tamils those days. National College of Lala Lajpat Rai was located in Lahore only. Bhagat Singh used to study there. Those days, it was considered as the cultural capital of the country. Even these days in the field of fine arts, a very famous play, written by Asgar Wazahat, with a title *"Jis Lahore Nahi Vekhya O Janmaya Hi Nahi"* gets staged very often, the title literary means a person who has not seen Lahore, is deemed to have not born. The height of love and intimacy that existed amongst these two cities ironically turned into depth of suffering with hatred and agony during partition days. During those days, pall of gloom used to descent on Amritsar whenever a train carrying dead bodies of Hindu families used to arrive from Pakistan. Similar pain might have been experienced at Lahore whenever train carrying dead bodies of Muslim families used to arrive from India. Those ghastly scars on minds of people had soured the relations between two nations, which still lingers on unabated. Bhagat Singh, Rajguru, and Sukhdev were hanged in the Lahore Jail. The pride of Undivided India – Lahore became part of Pakistan and Amritsar remained ours forever. In January 1995, I went to Amritsar for the first time. I had gone there in connection with a railway inspection. Upon entering Parcel Office, I asked where is Putlighar? An official said "it is nearby but what do you want?" I told him that I was looking for my friend Vivek Mahajan, a batch-mate during my training who was posted there. The official called for him and in the next five minutes, Vivek came to meet me there. With him, I moved around Amritsar and to Wagah Border. Amritsar is still connected with the old traditions and is a combination of old and new traditions. I never forget to bring *papad* and *vadi* from Amritsar.

Amritsar at one point of time was a part of Tung Village which was purchased by Sikh's 4th Guru Ramdas in 1574 for ₹ 700/- from the owners of Tung. Amritsar's name, in fact, is taken from Santokhsar Sarovar, which was built by Guru Ramdas by his own hands. Amritsar was made a city with four walls like Shahajahanabad of Delhi. Amritsar is connected with the Ramayana also. Amritsar is having Shri Ram Tirth Temple – it is an old *Ashram* of Rishi Valmiki. This temple is 11 kms away from Amritsar. As per Old story related with *Ramayan*, when Shri Ram had abandoned Sita ji, Valmiki gave shelter to Sitaji here. Here in this *Ashram*, Luv and Kush were born. Rishi Valmiki's hut and steps where Sitaji used to bathe are there.

located

Grand Trunk Road, which was made under the regime of Shershah Suri, passes through Amritsar. Once upon a time, Grand Trunk Road was going upto Bangladesh from Peshawar. In the present times, Amritsar is known for Golden Temple where people from all faiths from all over the world visit to pay regards and do holy *darshan*. This is also known as Harmandir Sahib, meaning temple of Hari. First stone for Harmandir Sahib was placed by Lahore's Sufi Saint Hazrat Miya Mirji as requested by Sikh's 5th Guru Arjun Dev ji. It was completed in 1604. *Langar* organised there is world-famous.

Fifth Guru of the Sikhs- Shri Guru Arjan Dev ji who laid down the Foundation of Golden Temple

In the Harmandir Sahib (Golden Temple) – everyday about 50,000 devotees participate in *Langar*. In the weekend and on festivals, this figure reaches about one lakh. *Langar* is served round the clock to devotees from all over the world. This practice was started by Sikh's 1st Guru Shri Guru Nanak Dev ji and the 3rd Guru Sh. Amar Das ji made it permanent.

There are two halls in the

Golden Temple where *Langar* is served to devotees.

In these halls, at a time, 5,000 people can take *Langar prasad*. In this *Langar*, daily 50 quintal flour, 18 quintal pulses, 14 quintal rice and seven quintal milk is consumed. 100 gas cylinders are required to prepare *Langar*. There is an automatic machine – (Roti Maker), which makes 25,000 *rotis* in an hour. In the hall, sanitation, hygiene and cleaning of utensils are given utmost importance. Used plates, glasses, etc. are washed in five stages and then only they are used again. All the devotees, irrespective of caste, class, and creed, are made to sit on the *chatais* (mats) running all along. Devotees from India and abroad derive immense happiness at the temple by offering *Sewa*.

In the nineteenth century, because of Afghan attack, Harmandir Sahib was destroyed heavily. Maharaja Ranjit Singh got it rebuilt with added grandeur of gold covering the main temple. Thus, it got the new name of Golden Temple (Swarna Mandir). The architectural map of this 400-year-old Gurudwara was prepared by Shri Arjun Dev ji personally. In this temple, there are four entrances. At that time, the society was divided into four castes. These four doors welcome everybody irrespective of caste and creed. There is no discrimination. In the premises of Harmandir Sahib, there is a tree of bair (berry), which is called 'Dukh Bhanjani Bair' (berry that removes all types of hardships). It is said that anybody getting its fruit – his/her all wishes get fulfilled and all difficulties are removed. It is also believed that anybody taking bath in Amritsar Sarovar below Dukh Bhanjani Bair is relieved from all sorrows and all moral wishes are fulfilled.

Author With Parents at Dukh-Bhanjini Beri in Golden Temple, Amritsar

I am the youngest amongst all the five siblings with an elder brother and three elder sisters. My grandmother was very keen that the family must have a pair of brothers. In the year 1974 my parents came to Golden Temple on pilgrimage and had prayed to fulfil their wish of getting another son under the same beri shrub. By the grace of the God and through the wish of my parents being granted, I was born the very next year. These days, also that "Dukh Bhanjan Bair" is present there, but has become fit weak.

In Amritsar, we have another grand Hindu temple known as Durgiana Temple. This is a famous shrine also known as Lakshmi Narayan Mandir, Shitla Mata Mandir and Durga Teerth. This is a Hindu Temple – its design resembles to Golden Temple Mandir. Devoted to Goddess Lakshmi and Lord Vishnu it is considered to be a very sacred temple. This was originally built in 16th century and was renovated into a grand temple in 1921 by Guru Harsai Mal Kapoor, which was then inaugurated by Pt. Madan Mohan Malviya.

Durgiana Temple Located at Amritsar

Here, I would like to talk about another great personality, Madan Lal Dhingra, who was born in an effluent family in Amritsar on 18th September, 1883. While studying in London, he had assassinated Sir William Hutt Curzon Wylli as one of the very first attempts at the start of the new phase of revolution. This incident had created quite a sensation in the country. He was associated with Shyam Ji Krishna

Revolutionary Madan Lal Dhingra

Verma and Veer Savarkar in the year 1906 at India House. In fact, he went to London for pursuing higher studies. His father was a reputed Civil Surgeon at Amritsar. Savarkar made Madan Lal a member of Abhinav Bharat – a revolutionary organisation and also trained him to use weapons. Dhingra used to stay in India House, which was the centre of activity for assembling the revolutionaries.

There was great discontent among them as one by one revolutionaries were being hanged and then when Curzon Wylli came to "India House" for attending a function on 1st July, 1909, Dhingra fired five rounds aimed at his face. At last, Madan Lal Dhingra was hanged on 17th August, 1909. His revolutionary activities were not liked by his father and he had denounced his relations with the son by getting notice published in the newspapers. A full-size statue of Madan Lal is placed in Amritsar and the Bus Terminal is also named after him.

Aman Ki Asha bus entering from Wagah Border into India

From Amritsar, the Pakistan border is only 28 kilometres. The place from where the entry and exit between two nations is there is known as 'Wagah Border'. After 1971 Pakistan War, Firozpur border was closed for business. Hence, Wagah became the centre for all business and political activities. Today also many commercial vehicles enter from this place. In the year

1999, the then PM Shri Atal Bihari Vajpayee had started a bus named 'Aman Ki Asha' for Pakistan. The bus service and other initiatives by India were taken in hope for peace (Aman ki Asha) but alas, these sincere efforts met with many acts of betrayal from Pakistan. Buses coming from Delhi to Lahore also pass through this route. Police vans escort this bus when it enters in India, so that it can reach Delhi safely.

At Wagah Border too, the ceremony of bringing down the flag (colour lowering) in evening is performed daily – an event which is witnessed by large number of people from both the countries. As compared with the similar ceremony at Firozpur, the programme conducted here is more gracious

Author along with friends at Wagah Border year 2000

and magnificent. The gaiety and enthusiasm displayed amongst the public is worth seeing with the aura of patriotism spread all around. The entire atmosphere is filled with the loud chants of 'Bharat Mata Ki Jai' and 'Vande Matram'. Just before Wagah Border, the last railway station of India is Attari. This is the last station on Indian side for trains plying into Pakistan. After Shimla Accord of 1972, train operation had commenced between India and Pakistan. In the beginning, rake of Pakistan Railway used to travel up to Delhi, but these days those rakes terminate at Atari itself.

Many eminent personalities were born in Amritsar – the prominent amongst them are Madan Lal Dhingra, singer Mohammad Rafi, first lady IPS Officer Kiran Bedi, cricketer Navjot Singh Sidhu, devotional singer Narendra Chanchal and India's first Field Marshal Sam Manekshaw. Field Marshal Manekshaw was a Parsi – how he came to be born in Amritsar is an interesting story, which will be narrated later in chapter of 1971 war.

After all these specialties of Amritsar, I should also tell you about its delicious food, so that whenever you visit there, you would relish them. *Chhole, tandoori kulche, kali dal* and *tandoori parathe* of two standout eating joints named *"Kesar da Dhaba"* and *"Bhrawan da Dhaba"* are very famous along with Sweets Fhirni of Bansal Sweets at Lawrence Road. In the desserts, fruit cream and kulfi of Hall Bazar are marvellous. It is up to you what to relish in the mouth-watering delicacies of Amritsar, but I would suggest you to taste the *Prasad* at the Golden Temple *Langar* without fail.

Hope that you will visit this city full of India's cultural heritage and will pay regards to the revolutionaries at Jallianwala Bagh.

□

5
KASHMIR AND 1947-48 WAR OF INDIA-PAKISTAN

Agar Firdaus Baroy Zamin Asta Hamiasto, Hamiasto, Hamiasto.!!

(Agar Dharti Par Kahi Swarg Hai To Yahi Hai, Yahi Hai, Yahi Hai...........)

– Amir Khusro (on the beauty of Kashmir)

As we all know that India got its independence on 15th August, 1947, but earlier to this our country was divided into 565 small Princely States (*Riyasaat*) ruled by kings and at the time of independence, all the erstwhile rulers had been granted with freedom to merge with either India or Pakistan or exercise the option of remaining independent by the British government. Sardar Patel was entrusted with the herculean task of getting them in Indian fold. He could manage to accomplish the challenging job to near perfection. Except for rulers of Junagarh and Hyderabad States, rulers of all other States had signed the consent Letter for their accession to India. Apart from these States, Goa was one such territory which came in India in the year 1961. But the issue of Kashmir accession remained pending, which was directly looked after by Nehruji, who being Kashmiri had a soft corner for Kashmir.

Before proceeding ahead, I will tell you about the history of Kashmir. Jammu-Kashmir was ruled by Dogra Kings for nearly 200 years. Jammu-Kashmir was the hindu-majority

State of India ruled by Hindu kings. The time moved on and a situation arose where Kashmiri Pandits were forcibly evicted from the Kashmir Valley and had to lead lives of refugees in their own motherland. Due to this unfortunate turn of events, Kashmiri Pandits have to endure the pathetic living in other States.

Author at World Famous Shalimar Bagh, Srinagar, 1999

Anyway, in the year 1947, the erstwhile Maharaja of Kashmir, Hari Singh refused to merge with either Pakistan or India. He had chosen to remain independent. But Pakistan had set its evil and cunning eye on Kashmir. Jinnah was confident that nothing could stop the merger of Kashmir with Pakistan. With such an evil design, he had sent Kabailis (tribal troups) to infiltrate into Kashmir for forcible possession. On 20th October, 1947, Pakistan gave weapons to *Pathans* and sent them along with Pak soldiers of its Army dressed as Kabaili to Kashmir for armed conflict.

Those Kabailis attacked Kashmir via Ebatabad-Muzaffarabad-Uri-Punch on 22nd October and entered into Baramula. They committed inhuman brutalities by not only killing people but also outraged the modesty of native women. Maharaja Hari Singh understood the cunningness of Pakistan and on 26th October, 1947, he signed consent for merger with India. The then Governor-General, Lord Mountbatten also approved the accession of Kashmir to India and this was made effective w.e.f. 27th October, 1947, there after Indian Army entered into Kashmir on the very day i.e. 27th October 1947.

It was clear instructions, of Pt. Nehru that before landing at Srinagar Air Strip, it must be ensured that no Pakistani Aircraft was on the airfield there. So, Air Force Pilot, Patnaik brought Lt. Col. Ranjit Roy along with his 17 soldiers to the airfield by making two sorties and ensuring no Pakistani aircraft was at the field.

After this, Lt. Col. Ranjit Roy started his arduous work of saving Baramula. Kabailis again attacked and injured Lt. Col. Roy, who later succumbed to his injuries. He was the first officer to have sacrificed his life for Kashmir. On 2nd November, Brig. Sen was deployed at the Kashmir Valley. India's brave Army saved Srinagar Airport and all-out efforts to throw the enemy out of Valley were launched with full might. Lastly, U.N.O. passed a resolution for ceasefire in the region. After that, many a time Pakistani Army tried to intrude and wage war, but on all such misadventures were thwarted by our victorious Indian Army. The ceasefire resulted in a status quo situation, where 34% area of J&K remained under the control of Pakistan, which now is known as Pakistan Occupied Kashmir (POK) which actually is our integral part according to the accession pact signed by King of Jammu & Kashmir Sh. Hari Singh.

During this war, a very brave officer of our Indian Army deserves a special mention as a commander, who was lured by Jinnah to change his loyalties to Pakistan and use his military acumen as General of Pakistan Army. The brave officer referred to here was one of most gallant sons produced by Mother India, Brigadier Mohd. Usman, who

Brigadier Mohammad Usman

flatly refused the tempting offer of becoming Chief of Army Staff of Paskistan Army and preferred to serve India with utmost devotion and loyalty. At the promising age of 36 years, he had sacrificed all he had including life for the cause of the country.

When he refused the offer, Jinnah got irritated and announced a reward of ₹ 50,000/- to anyone who would bring his head. You can imagine that the amount of ₹ 50,000/- was a staggering huge fortune at that time. Brigadier Usman laid down his life while conquering the battle of Naushera. He is the only Brigadier-ranked officer of Indian Army who laid down his life while fighting actively. Generally, officers of such high rank plan and manage strategies of warfare and are not required to participate in the active field. He not only went out to join the fight but also slept with his soldiers on the ground. He was born on 15th July, 1912 at Mau, Uttar Pradesh and martyred in Kashmir on 3rd July, 1948. Because of his exemplary show of ultimate bravery, he is also known as "Naushera Ka Sher". His body was buried at Jamia Milia Islamia, Delhi and in his burial ceremony, then Prime Minister Pt. Nehru and Abul Kalam Azad had also participated. I also got an opportunity to pay homage to him at his grave.

It is not possible that while talking about the War of 1947, we don't mention the name of Major Somnath Sharma for his amazing contribution. Despite having fractured his hand while playing hockey, he successfully saved Badgam area from going into the hands of Kabailis, but in this great endeavour, he had made the supreme sacrifice of his life. Before his death a message was sent to Headquarters –

Major Somnath Sharma

"Enemy is only 50 yards away from us but we will not go back by even an inch." In addition to the great contribution by Major Sharma, we also had vital contributions from other war heroes like Company Havaldar Major Peeru Singh Shekhawat, Lance Naik Karam Singh, Naik Jadunath Singh and 2nd Lt. Ram Raghoba Rane. All of them were awarded with Param Veer Chakra for their unmatched valour and bravery.

In the independent India, Major Somnath Sharma was the first to receive Param Veer Chakra. The highest gallantry award of India, Param Veer Chakra was instituted on 26th January, 1950 and Major Sharma was its first recipient. Due to the heroic deeds of Somnath ji and

Beautiful view of Baltal from Zojila Pass

Lance Naik Karam Singh

his soldiers, Srinagar Airbase was saved. For paying him homage, his statue is placed at the entry of Srinagar Airport.

Zozila Pass was an important place during 1947 War between Kabailis and Indian Army. Indian Army used tanks at such a greater height which has never happened in any part of the world.

In July 1999, when I was passing through Zozila Pass, there were still mounds of snow left at few places. My dreams were coming true. In the year 1948, when Pakistanis were determined not to move away from here, Gen. Carriappa (at that time, he was Chief of Western Command as Lt. Col.) made a plan. All the tanks were dismantled, brought them to Baltal in trucks, reassembled there and were used in the ensuing warfare. Brigadier Hira Lal Atal had implemented the plan drawn by Gen. Carriappa. Enemy could not have dreamt of anything like this. The shocked Pakistani forces were forced to withdraw from Zozila, Dras, and Kargil. At such a greater height, tanks were never used. Excellent camouflage was used to keep the transportation of tanks through trucks a top secret, curfew was imposed in the areas falling on the route to prevent any leakage of information.

Field Marshal K.M. Cariappa

Zozila Pass remains closed for six winter months even these days and thus rendering Leh disconnected with mainland of the country for these six months. Government of India is constructing an 'All-Weather Road', which will be completed very soon. Government is spending ₹ 10,050 crores on this project. Then it will be possible to reach Leh by road throughout the year. From strategical point of view, it is an important work which will help augment security of country.

I wish in addition to this road link, if Leh-Manali route is also made all-weather, it would be nice. It is commonly believed that travelling from Manali to Leh by road provides for the ultimate joyful experience due to the picturesque sites all along the road. If this route is developed, it will be a great step strategically and also boost tourism immensely. From Aksai Chin side, China tries to infiltrate and it will be easy for the Indian Army to reach there to foil these attempts. Apart from this, in Himanchal Pradesh, there are many border areas near China. Their aggressive designs can be thwarted effectively by having this all-weather road. Recently, it was in the news that the government was trying to bring rail upto there. If that be the case, it will be an effective step to counter Chinese invasion.

Kashmir Valley stood as a proud witness of sacrifices made by Brigadier Mohammad Usman, Major Somnath Sharma and Lt. Ranjit Roy. In the war of Jammu-Kashmir, total of about 6,000 soldiers either lost their lives or got injured. Out of these, 1,500 soldiers became martyrs, 3,500 were injured and 1,000 went missing and were not traceable. In this war, 5 Param Veer Chakras, 53 Mahavir Chakras, and 323 Veer Chakras were awarded.

□

6
1962 INDO-CHINA WAR

Ae Mere Vatan Ke Logo, Zara Ankh Me Bhar Lo Paani,
Jo Shaheed Hue Hain Unki Zara Yaad Karo Kurbaani!
– Kavi Pradeep

We all are aware that Leh-Ladakh is the land of many passes (*Darrey*). It is the highest plateau of Jammu-Kashmir and is a cold desert. Chushul was the centre of 1962 War, whereas Leh is located at the height of above 11,000 feet from sea level, Chushul is at above 14,231 feet. At many places, the height is between 15,000 and 17,000 feet. China, for many years had been constructing roads and Army Posts till the advent of year 1963. Our leaders had blind faith in comradeship of China and ignored these signals by turning blind eyes to those activities. Then, the unimaginable act of back-stabbing took place and our worse fears proved to be true. China attacked us on 20th October, 1962. Major Dhansingh Thapa (1/8 Gorkha Rifles) was entrusted with the security of a part of this challenging area. Major Thapa and his soldiers valiantly gave a befitting reply to the Chinese. Although, in the face of high degree of preparedness by China, our prospects of victory were negligible, yet Major Dhansingh Thapa and his troop fought with bravery and remained at the post trying to hold fort till the last. Chinese soldiers took him as Prisoner of War and tried very hard through torture to elicit vital military information but could not succeed. At last, Chinese forces released him. For his gallantry, he was awarded with Param Veer Chakra.

The responsibility of securing another area of Chushul was entrusted to Major Shaitan Singh. Little away from Chushul, at 18,000 feet height, Rejang La is situated. Strategically, it was a very important post like Chushul. Here our soldiers were led by Major Shaitan Singh. A resident of Jodhpur in Rajasthan, Major Shaitan Singh was posted with 13th Kumaon Regiment. On 18th November, 1962 when Chinese attack was in full swing, Major and his soldiers gave a befitting reply to advances made by the Chinese Army.Major suffered with serious injuries, but even then he kept encouraging his soldiers to fight on. After fighting bravely against the enemy, he made the supreme sacrifice of his life.

Major Dhan Singh Thapa

All of a sudden, snowfall started and his body got buried in the snow. After three months, when snow started reducing, his body was taken out cremation with full state honours was done at Chushul. Major Shaitan Singh was awarded posthumously with Param Veer Chakra. Other brave soldiers like Naik Hukum Chand, Naik Gulab Singh Yadav, Lance Naik Ram Singh, Subedar Ram Kumar, and Subedar Ram Chander were awarded with Veer Chakra.

Major Shaitan Singh

The war of Rejang La was regared as one of the most unique wars in the martial history as the deployed strength of only 124 Indian soldiers (out of which 114 were killed) had inflicted very heavy casualty on China by having killed 1,310 Chinese soldiers with the display of unmatched fighting skills and outstanding courage. Even the Chinese armymen were also impressed with such courageous fightback.

In September 2016, after paying our homage to martyrs at Siachen Base Camp, we proceeded for Chushul via a road adjacent to Pagong Tso Lake. There is a short-cut created through a rough and unpaved road. It took us about three hours to travel a distance of only 45 kms. On the way, we had seen many posts of ITBP (Indo- Tibet Border Police). Supervisor of ITBP Force, apprised us about the area. Prior to 1962 War, the entire lake belonged to us, but nowadays only 30% of the lake area remains with us and the remaining has been taken by China. On the way to Chushul, we saw Dhansingh Thapa Post. This post is named after Param Veer Chakra recipient Dhansingh Thapa. In the 1962 War, Dhansingh Thapa was posted there. At that time, it was known as Thakum Post.

Milestone Located at Chushul outside the rest house of ITBP

In the Pagong Lake area, Indian Army and ITBP both have their own ultramodern motor boats Army has acquired even bulletproof motor boats from USA. They are capable to counter the enemy attack.

By the time we reached ITBP Rest House at Chushul it was pitch dark and had become very cold. The jawan posted at mess offered us with piping-hot momos and hot tea. Thereafter, Asstt. Commandant Rakesh Kumar showed us the Chinese border and told us about Chushul and Rezang La. He informed us that China suffered a great loss here and Major Shaitan Singh had thrown the Chinese into a tizzy. It is said that because of lesser number of weapons and ammunition, he was ordered to recede back but still then he decided to fight and his soldiers followed him.

In the night, the temperature was very low and I could not sleep due to the cold. The temperature was zero in the month of September. Spare a thought as to how cold it would have been in November, when Major Shaitan Singh and his troop fought valiantly.

In the morning, we could see a novel way of paying homage – a post was named after his wife Tara & Hina Post after the name of his daughter and Rohit Post was named after his son.

Rohit, son of Shaitan Singh, went on to become a Brigadier in the Indian Army. He still serving in Indian Army, following the tradition of which his grandfather and father were honourable members. After coming out of Guest House, we proceeded towards open ground where on one side our posts are located and on the other side Chinese area was clearly visible. In the first place, we prayed at War Memorial of Gorkha Regiment. After 20 kms drive, we reached Rezang La where memorial is made for 114 soldiers who laid their lives smilingly in national service. They all were cremated

War Memorial of Gorkha Regiment Located at Chushul

on this ground only. From the war field, 114 stones were brought here so that their memory remains with us. The name of these martyrs of 13th Kumaun are written in golden letters in our history. We will never be able to pay back their debts.

At this memorial, we became emotional with our heart filled with immense sense of gratitude. Recently, the National Book Trust has brought comics for children on Shaitan Singh's bravery so that the coming generation could know them and pay regards. In the Jodhpur Division of Indian Railways, a station is named Shaitan Singh Nagar, dedicated to his memory.

On the memorial of Rezang La, few lines by poet Thomas Macaulay are written – "How can a man die better than facing fearful odds for the ashes of his fathers and the temples of his gods." Here I would like to mention that the following places are marked for the meeting of Indian and Chinese Forces:

1. Chushul: Leh, Jammu-Kashmir
2. Nathu La: Sikkim
3. Boom La: Tawang, Arunachal Pradesh
4. Lipulekh Pass: Uttarakhand

Author with friends at Rejang la war Memorial

After seeing Leh in 2007, the only desire was to see Tawang – which also got fulfilled in October 2014.

After 1962 War, China illegally has occupied our 42,735 sq. km area`of Aksai Chin and Arunachal Pradesh. It is a known fact that this war was the most drastic and destructive for us in which we have not only lost our land but also lost our brave soldiers in large numbers. The responsibility of all these goes to policies made by Pt. Nehru and then Defence Minister Krishna Menon. Menon Sahib got many ordinance factories of arms and ammunition closed under the pretext that India would not be threatened by any other foreign country. Not only this, he also got defence budget allocations reduced drastically. Such irrational thinking became the prime cause for our defeat in 1962 – the defeat which hurts us even these days. When China took Tibet under its control, Sardar Patel wrote a long letter to Pt. Nehru, warning him to be cautious against the tactics of China. In December 1950, Sardar Patel had passed away and Nehru, who was an ardent follower of Panchsheel, forget Patel's warning. Had India taken that warning in the right earnest, the result of Indo-China conflict in 1962 could have been entirely different.

Apart from this warning from Patel, there were many other indications of imminent danger of the Chinese aggression lurking at India observed during the years 1960 and 1961. Even then Nehru ji and Menon could not wake up from their deep slumber to the imminent risks from China. The fact that the Army Chief General Thimayya was not having cordial relations with Menon also aggravated the problem. The entire country had to suffer for their omissions and misjudgements for decades and even till today. The preparation standard at the military level was so abysmal that when it went to capture Goa, a Battalion was equipped with canvass shoes. China War was fought by Indian Army with 303 Bolt Action Guns, whereas China was having AK 47 guns. In the year 2016, I got to read a book written by Kunal Verma titled *1962: The War That Was Not* in which entire details were described by the writer's father who was Captain in Indian Army in the year 1962. This book is an eye-opener as to what difficulties were faced by our soldiers because of Nehru ji and Krishna Menon.

On 17th November, 1962, when Chinese Army entered into Nuranag, Rifleman of Garhwal Rifles, Jaswant Singh with his two accompanying soldiers, Lance Naik Trilok Singh and Rifleman Gopal Singh held the fort against the invaders. In fact, Chinese soldiers had entered Arunachal Pradesh from three sides of Bum La Pass. One group coming from the side of Se La Pass was stopped by Jaswant Singh and his soldiers. The other Chinese groups managed to reach upto Tejpur. In this conflict, China had lost its 300 soldiers. When they attacked fourth time, Jaswant Singh, who was moving to get a machine gun of a dead Chinese soldier, was hit by a bullet and was injured seriously. Jaswant Singh alone had been fighting for the last 72 hours. The room where he was staying has now been converted into a small temple. Today also, bedsheet

Rifleman Jaswant Singh Rawat

A Statue at the entrance gate of Jaswant Singh war Memorial Located at Arunachal Pradesh

is changed everyday. Five soldiers serve him day and night. Indian Army considers him as alive and has given him five promotions. Every soldier, higher official of Indian Army passing through there cannot go ahead without saluting Jaswant Singh – who now from Rifleman has become Captain. There is another speciality of that place. Every passerby is served with hot tea. Delicious samosa can also be relished there for ₹ 5 only. Here few bunkers are still maintained by Indian Army. In them phones, utensils, helmets, etc. which were used by those soldiers, have been displayed. We were told that these bunkers were made within 23 days. Chinese force started infiltration in September 1962. At that time, Indian Army had erected these bunkers. There can't be two opinions on the fact that China betrayed the trust deposed in them by India in 1962. The real reasons for losing the war can never be attributed to Indian Army, but the political leadership of those days was to be blamed for the faith reposed in Chinese leadership. After visiting relevant places, it is observed that there was no dearth of gallantry in our force – many of them sacrificed their lives. The war with China went upto 20th November, 1962 for one month from 20th October. Thereafter,

A board in memory of Rifleman Jaswant Singh Rawat at Jaswant Garh, Arunachal Pradesh

Inner View of Jaswant Singh War Memorial

China had announced ceasefire unilaterally.

Author at Sela Pass, Arunachal Pradesh

During the war there was acute paucity of resources for our Indian soldiers. They were not having woolen clothing. A single blanket was used by four jawans. Many of them had died because of harsh weather and inadequate protection against it. Leave alone the lack of woolen clothing, they did not even possess requisite weapons. Main reason for our debacle was paucity of weapons and more primarily, the inept handling and insensitive attitude of Defence Minister and Prime Minister. This is still beyond imagination why Pt. Nehru did not use Air Force – otherwise also Chinese Air Force could not have reached Tibet. America later on confirmed this fact. During discussions in Parliament on Chinese War, Nehru ji informed that 42,735 sq. km. area, which was captured by China, is totally barren and useless. On this statement, one MP Shri Mahavir Tyagi sarcastically commented that he being bald and did not have any hair left on his head. By the same standard, he should also be handed over to China. China has illegally captured 42,735 sq. km. of our land which is sufficient in carving out 28 Delhi-size States.

The boundary dispute between India and China had proved to be Achilles tendon since the year 1914, when British Government entered into an agreement with China recognising Mac Mahon Line as the demarcation of boundary. Communist Government of China then in 1949 had its apprehension about it and doubted it to be against their interest and, hence, was reluctant to whole-heartedly recognise it. Whereas, India was under the impression that China will follow Mac Mahon Line. Dalai Lama, the crusader against tyranny of China, left strife torn Tibet on exile to India and initially stayed at Tawang before coming to Delhi where he was accorded with a warm welcome by Nehru. This incident irked the Chinese Government. India should have been alerted by their resentment but our then leaders instead were busy welcoming Chinese leadership too. It was Nehru who advocated in United Nations to provide China with permanent membership in Security Council in the year 1960. I have been fortunate enough to have offered my respect and homage to martyrs of Nuranag.

Just like Nuranag, we have a small region known as Tawang. Although the place is small, yet it is very significant due to its strategically important location. It is located very near to the Chinese boundary. Tawang was a vital sector during the 1962 War and China at times claims Tawang to be its territory. When one goes about 50 km upward in north from Tawang, there is a place named 'Bumla' – from here Chinese land can be seen. This, in fact, is LAC (Line of Actual Control) which separates India and China. In the year 1962, Chinese had entered from this point. Subedar Joginder Singh of 1st Sikh Regiment was posted here. We have already discussed about the scarcity of arms and ammunition with our military, same was the

Tawang War Memorial, Arunachal pradesh

Another view of Tawang War Memorial

case here also for which the post had to pay very dearly by conceding defeat. Chinese attacked this post on 23rd October, 1962, although our soldiers were with far fewer in numbers, yet definitely not on courage. The high degree of courage is evident from the fact that despite having only 17 soldiers left in command of Subedar Joginder Singh, he did not give up and charged bravely on to the invading swarm of soldiers with a war cry of *'Jo bole so Nihal, Sat Sri Akaal'*. He received numerous injuries but he could save his post from the first invasion. But could not ward of second attack. When cartridges got exhausted, he faught valiantly with the butt of the gun, till the time he breathed his last, in service of our motherland. A memorial for his brave defiance has been raised at the post.

Sardar Joginder Singh

After that war, the situation on these fronts has largely remained calm as guns on both sides have mostly gone silent except for a few stray incidents. At this post, Indian Army has a conference room, a guest house and a small auditorium.

Param Vir Chakra Joginder Singh Memorial Bum La, Arunachal Pradesh

These days, Chinese soldiers conduct dinner parties for our soldiers every year on 1st and 30th October. They erect a tent for the lavish party in front of this post in their area of control. In a similar gesture, Indians invite Chinese to join celebration parties on the occasions of 15th August and 26th January. This tradition has been followed year after year. A Major deployed at post briefed us that in 1962 War, Chinese had invaded from this area. These days the dividing line between two countries is signified as "Rock of Peace". We experienced problem in breathing at the height of 16,000 feet at Bumla. There was slight snowfall also during our visit. It was very cold and despite wearing four layers of warm clothes, I was experiencing too much of cold. We were surprised to see that there was road upto last post of China, whereas, on our side, no such infrastructure was there. Here electricity was

Author with a friend Mukesh at Indo-China Border, Bum La Pass

available through a generator – that too upto 3 p.m. There was no mobile connectivity. When we checked our mobile, WiFi signals were available from Chinese side. It shows that the provisions made by China is far better than us and we could not even make the roads. This realisation was painful for us. During my visit to Leh in 2007, I could see that the arrangements at Pakistan Border were comparatively better, maybe because Pakistan poses greater threat as copared to China in the list of our enemies. Being Army's guest, we were treated at Army Guest House with hot *Paranthas* and Potato *Sabzi*. Such delicious treat by our Army at the height of 16,000 feet was unimaginable. Hot tea provided us with great energy.

At Tawang, we paid homage at War Memorial and after offering our gratitude to martyrs, proceeded back towards Guwahati.

In the War of 1962, Major Shaitan Singh, Subedar Joginder Singh and Major Dhansingh Thapa were awarded the highest gallantry award Param Veer Chakra.

Every Indian during his lifetime should visit for once areas like Chushul and Tawang so that they can see how our soldiers have sacrificed their lives and do away with all comforts. During this war, 1,383 soldiers became martyrs, 1,047 were injured, 1,696 were not traceable and 3,968 were taken as Prisoners of War.

□

7

1965 INDO-PAK WAR

The safety, honour and welfare of your country come first, always and every time. The honour, welfare and comfort of the men you command come next. Your own ease, comfort and safety come last, always and every time.

– Lord Philip Chetwode

In the year 1965, Pakistan attacked India under an impression that India must have not forgotten the wounds inflicted on it in the 1962 War with China and would not have yet recovered from the jolt. The death of Pt. Nehru in 1964 also had further strengthened its unfounded beliefs. Pakistan thought that this was the opportune time to attack India to get Kashmir merged with Pakistan. There was one more reason of that misadventure. At that time Pakistan was playing in the hands of USA. They were not only getting weapons from USA but were also getting open support on all the fronts. USA had provided highly modern Patton tanks to Pakistan. India's tanks were technologically no match to those Patton tanks as we had very old Sharman tanks used in Second World War. At that time, Pakistan was having 756 tanks in which 352 were Patton – whereas India was having 608 tanks in which 182 were Centurian and others were Sharmans. Not only tanks but Pakistan possessed modern weapons also. There is an old saying in Hindi – "Dushman ka Dushman Dost" (Enemy's enemy is a friend) – to prove this right, Bhutto the then foreign minister of Pakistan approached China. He taking advantage of strained relations between India and China made concrete efforts to bring China with them. Since then, the closeness of China and Pakistan has been increasing; nowadays the scenario is such that Pakistan has given permission to China to make road in Pakistan Occupied Kashmir (PoK) and also on its own land. On the other hand, China, with a view to get business and trade advantage, has taken land from Pakistan at Gwadar Port and connected it directly from Aksai Chin, so that the oil and other goods from Gulf countries can be brought quickly and economically to China. All this is done by these countries under the aegis of CPEC (CHINA PAKISTAN ECONOMIC CORRIDOR). In the future, China is planning to connect Karachi and Peshawar cities with Chinese areas. It seems that China by doing all these wants to keep a closer watch on India and also to pressurise India on strategic fronts. All these activities concern India. India will have to make a policy in this regard quickly. India has already started working on that. Recently, by the move of Indian Army, deploying "Brahmos" Missiles at Indo-China Border, has made China anxious.

Anyway, Let's come back to the 1965 War. Pakistan's wrong understanding of 1965 situations had created havoc for it, quite like a self-goal. This planning of war was said to be conceived by the then Foreign Minister of Pakistan Zulfiqar Ali Bhutto. He made President Ayub Khan to believe in the plan that if Pakistan attacks India, it would not only teach a lesson to India but also benefit them by winning Kashmir. Ayub Khan agreed with the plans of Bhutto, thinking that India after debacle in 1962 War must not be prepared to fight and might have been rendered psychologically weak.

This war was started by Pakistan from Rann of Kutch in Gujarat. They were trying to see the reaction of India and were also trying to attract our attention towards Kutch as a distraction, so that they can easily infiltrate in Kashmir. Pakistan started it from Sardar Post at Kutch – it is a fact that Central Reserve Police Force had completely crushed and foiled their attack in a fight lasting just 12 hours. Despite the technological superiority of Pakistan military that had improved tanks and aircraft, Indian Army with its exemplary dedication, high morale, and unmatched courage dismantled their evil intentions. This war was fought with a new strategy with a paradigm shift in approach where Indian forces were allowed to enter Pakistan and carry out all-out attack on them. Undoubtedly, Lal Bahadur Shastri a was a stubborn and courageous PM, although possessed small physical frame. He ordered our Army to give more than a befitting reply to the enemy. When Army Chief J.N. Chaudhary told Shastriji that we will have to strike enemy in its own house – Shastriji approved readily. This was somehow strange deviation in our policy as India had never before this raided to violate International Boundary.

Despite we were having Britain's Centurian and Sharman Tanks used in Second World War and Pakistan was having modern and improved Patton – Pakistan could not have imagined the destructive fate their Patton Tanks met at the hands of competitive Indian Army.

In the War of 1965, following have brave personnel stood out for having shown exemplary courage:

1. At Hazi Pir – Lt. Col. Ranjeet Singh Dayal
2. At Fillora – Lt. Col. A.B. Tarapore and Major Bhupinder Singh
3. At Asal Uttar – Company Qtr. Master Havaldar Abdul Hamid
4. At Barki – Subedar Ajit Singh
5. At Dograi – Lt. Col. Desmond Hayde, Major ASA RAM TYAGI & Captain Kapil Singh Thapa.

Lieutenant General Ranjit Singh Dayal

Indian Soldiers at Barki near Lahore, Pakistan

Entry point for Pakistan's kabailis was from Hazi Peer and it was important for India to plug it completely. This assignment of plugging the entry through Hazi Peer was given to Major Ranjeet Singh Dayal of Para Troopers (he went on to become Lt. General later). He carried out the responsibility efficiently. To achieve this, the soldiers had to depend on dry food articles, like biscuits and namkeen for many days continually and also were required to conquer adverse climatic conditions at a great height. Soldiers under the leadership of Ranjeet Dayal had not given up and took a firm control over the Hazi Peer. For his display of stupendous gallantry, Ranjeet Singh Dayal was awarded with Mahaveer Chakra. But, later on, because of Tashkent Agreement, India and Pakistan were required to vacate the occupied areas and respect the sanctity of Line of Control (LOC). Our soldiers were agonised to vacate Hazi Peer as many of their fellow soldiers had sacrificed their lives for winning that.

Indian Soldiers after capturing Barki Police Station

In January 2017 I got a chance to meet two

Lieutenant Colonel A.B. Tarapore

distinguished war heroes of 1965 war namely Lt. Gen. A.N. VARMA & Brig. Aruinder Singh. At a book release function of Ms. Rachna Bisht Rawat who herself belong to family of Armymen. She has authored a book on "1965 title 1965 - Bharat Pakistan Yudh ki veer gathayian." It was originally written in the year 2015 & published by Ministry of defence to commemorate victory of 1965 war. Original title of the book in english is "1965 - Stories from the reand Indo Pak war".

In the war of 1965, Indian Tricolour was also furled at Barki in Pakistan which is just 15 kms away from Lahore. This feat was accomplished under the able leadership of Subedar Ajit Singh. I have already told you about Barki Memorial at Firozpur.

Here it is necessary to mention the name of Lt. Col. Tarapore who with his courage and bravery had won this battle. Tarapore was born in Bombay, (present day Mumbai). Tarapore – belonged to Pune Horse was instructed to capture Fillora on 11th September, 1965. In the Sialkot area of Pakistan at Fillora, he fought bravely riding on a Centurian Tank. Not caring about his injuries and wounds, he fought till India's win and at last, he sacrificed his life. Posthumously, he was awarded with Param Veer Chakra. He and his troop had destroyed 60 tanks of Pakistan. Tarapore at the age of 42 was seniormost in age to have received Param Veer Chakra. Major Bhupinder Singh was also awarded with Mahavir Chakra. Major Bhupinder Singh was from the same Armed Regiment which destroyed 27 tanks of enemy. Major Singh was badly injured and at last he succumbed to his injuries. In his name, at West Delhi a colony is named – Major Bhupinder Singh Nagar.

Asal Uttar region was literally turned into graveyard

for the enemies by the heroic deeds of Company Quarter Master Havaldar Abdul Hamid. He was born on 1st July, 1933 at a place named Dhamupur in Ghazipur district of Uttar Pradesh. Abdul Hamid, possessing a towering height of 6 feet 2 inches, had been very keen to do something great for our country. Before joining Army, he did tailoring job of stitching clothes. At the age of 14 years, he was married to Rasoolan Bibi. They had five children – one daughter and four sons. His dream came true when a recruitment camp was arranged at his village. He was pained for not being able to do something for the country in the 1962 War and was always thinking to do something worthwhile. In 1962 war, he was deployed at NEFA – (Thegh La). On 10th September, 1965, he was deployed at Khemkaran Sector with his Regiment-4 Grenadiers, where he was in his jeep which was fitted with a Mobile Rocket Launcher (R.C.L. Gun) targeting enemy's Patton Tanks. He destroyed seven Patton Tanks of the enemy and then enemy targeted him – he breathed his last on 10th September, 1965. For his gallantry, he was awarded with Param Veer Chakra. In this war, where Pakistan took possession of 540 sq. kms of Indian lands, the Indian Army took control of 1940 sq. kms. of Pakistan.

Abdul Hamid Memorial Located at Asal Uttar, Punjab

At Asal Uttar, where Abdul Hamid had sacrificed his life, Indian Army has made a Martyrs' Memorial. There is his *Mazar*, where thousands come regularly to pay their homage. In the year 2015, Prime Minister Shri Narendra Modi has paid homage there. This place is not less than a *Pawan Teerth* (sacred pilgrimage) and every Indian should

Inner View of Abdul Hamid Memorial Located at Asal Uttar

go there at least for once. Asal Uttar is located at a distance of 60 kms. only from Amritsar and is well connected with main parts of country. At Asal Uttar, the then Lt. Gen. Harbux Singh designed a unique strategy in which agricultural fields were flooded with water fetched from canal. Patton Tanks had to be grounded like toys. Near Asal Uttar, a graveyard of tanks had been created and 97 Pakistani Patton Tanks were lined up there. In the history of wars worldwide, such a large-scale destruction of tanks en masse is one of its kind and never heard of before.

In the same manner at Dograi, three Jats under the leadership of Lt. Col. Desmond Hayde, Indian Army gained coveted victory. War at Dograi is considered to be one amongst the most difficult wars fought by Indian Army. Hayde's encouragement to each and every soldier was so effective that every soldier became prepared mentally to sacrifice his life. Lt. Col. told two things to his soldiers – "Nobody will go back" and "Dead or alive will meet tomorrow at Dograi". So much was the impact of this that we won the battle. Lt. Col. Desmund was awarded

Lieutenant General Harbaksh Singh

with Mahaveer Chakra. After retirement, he has settled at Kotdwar. He wrote a poem for children—

"Kadam badha ke chal, Sur mila ke chal,
Aandhiyon se na tu dagmaga, sach ki raho pe chal!!"

In Dograi two other officer from LAT regiment Major ASA RAM TYAGI & Captain Kapil Singh Thapa were also awarded with Mahaveer Chakra for dislaying exemplary courage. In one morning of July 2016, I got an opportunity to pay homage to Martyr Sukhdev at his ancestral house at Nau Ghara Chauda Bazar. At Ludhiana, one more patriotic personality was born, named Kartar Singh Sarabha. His one big statue is placed on G.T. Road. After his *darshan*, when we were proceeding towards Khemkaran and Asal Uttar – my mind was occupied by the series of scenes plying like a documentary as to how great Abdul Hamid might have destroyed so many Pakistani tanks. On the way, a Bridge hust had passed by. With curiosity, I asked the driver of our vehicle – is this place Harike? He nodded in affirmative. I asked the driver to stop the car. Just under the bridge, I could see the magnificent view of Beas River merging with Satluj. Beas River originates from Beas Kund at Rohtang Pass, Himanchal Pradesh. As per a religious story, this river originated as a result of 12 years of deep devotional meditation by Maharshi Ved Beas. Its water is considered to be very pious. While coming back from Ladakh, we had *darshan* of Vyas Kund. I don't really know the reasons for my fascination of seeing confluence of rivers, they look very beautiful to my eyes. Till now, I got opportunity to see both origins as well as points of their merger of Ganga, Yamuna, Beas, Narmada, and Indus Rivers.

Author at Indo-Pak Khemkaran Border, Punjab

After crossing the Harike, we reached at *Mazar* (grave memorial) of brave Abdul Hamid. This was the same Cheema Village where Abdul Hamid had turned the battle in our favour. After paying our homage there, we went to Khemkaran, to see Border Observation Post number 191 geographically it in the last part of India. When we climbed on to the top of this observation tower and had looked below at the vast expanse of surrounding, we were quite amazed with the view. It is quite amazing as to how our soldiers carry out vigil on the border land the clock. Pakistan's Post located was at a very sh t distance of about 100 yards from here. At that time, we were at the end of Indian Road which is now closed with the help of bricks. Pakistan's Kasur district starts from here on the other side of the boundary.

Fencing has been put up on border by India to prevent any attempts of infiltration into our area. In the night, Section 144 is imposed and electric current passes through that fencing. Despite so many arrangements made at the border, sporadic incidents of smuggling the drugs and arms occur. In the decade of nineties, the fencing was not provided. Probably due to this reason, Sarabjeet had strayed into the area of Pakistan and was imprisoned for 22 years in the Kot Lakhpat Jail of Lahore. Recently, I got a chance to see the movie made on the life of Sarabjeet, it really shaken me and I was forced to think how Pakistan with uncalled-for cruelty and insensitiveness had ruined the life of a

Author at Indo-Pak border Khemkaran

simple man. We had planned to go via Bhikhivind, which is Sarabjeet's village, on our way to Amritsar. I decided to meet Sarabjeet's brave sister Dalbir Kaur personally to convey my regards for the untiring efforts made by her for securing release of Sarabjeet.

After seeing this post, we went to a *dargah* of a *Peer Shaikh Brahma* which is situated on the No Man's Land or Zero Line. Visit to that place is permitted on Thursdays only and that too after having to undergo rigorous frisking. Here at his *dargah*, not only Indians but even Pakistanis also come to pray. The white pole separating India and Pakistan is only four steps away from the place where we had prayed. It is said that Guru Nanak Dev ji during his Mecca entourage had come there. In my entire life, I have seen this *dargah* as the only one where big bells have been provided. Nobody is permitted to stay there. One very big *deepak* (earthern lamp) is placed there which is lit continuously. Thereafter, we reached at the house of Sarabjeet. His sister-in-law was present there, who informed us that the family had gone to Jullundhur for attending a function. She told us that after the release of the film on his life, many people have started visiting them. After praying for the well-being of the family, we started for Amritsar. There we bowed down at Golden Temple and by night train from Amritsar reached Delhi in the morning.

Dargah of Peer Sheikh Brahm Ji at Khemkaran Border

In the 1965 War, if the reference of the then Air Chief is not made, the narrative would remain incomplete. During the 1965 War, Indian Air Force was headed by Sardar Arjan Singh. Air Chief Marshal Arjan Singh was born on 15th April, 1919 at Layalpur, Punjab (at present, Faislabad, Pakistan). He received his elementary education at Montgomery (now in Pakistan). In 1938, he took admission in Royal Air Force College, Krainwell and in 1939, he was commissioned in IAF as Pilot Officer. He was Air Chief from 1st August, 1964 to 15th July, 1969. Because of his important contribution in the 1965 War, he was made India's first and only Marshall of the Indian Air Force. He had served as Lt. Governor of Delhi from December 1989 to December 1990. He was a proven leader who motivated generation of officers and men of Air Force. He has passed away in September, 2017 at the age of 98 years.

Now I will tell you about an officer who not only wrote new stories of patriotism but has been a hero, a real role model for today's generation. This great officer is none other than Major Haripal Singh Ahluwalia. Major Ahluwalia was the member of Everest Expedition Team of India. On 29th May, 1965, he conquered the Mount Everest and got orders for joining war duties in September. He fought bravely but one bullet hit him in spine – compelling him to be on wheel chair since then. With the great courage and indomitable spirit, he accepted this challenge and established Indian Spine Injury Hospital at Vasant Kunj in Delhi, where patients with spine damage are treated. For his resolute determination, he had been conferred with many coveted awards, such as Padma Bhushan, Padma Shree and Arjuna Awards. Till this date, Ahluwalia Sahib has written 13 books. In the year 1998, I had read his autobiography *Higher than Everest* – since then I have become his ardent fan. Thrice I have met him personally. Not only this, my second book *Atulya Bharat Ki Khoj* has been blessed by him.

In the 1965 Indo-Pak War, 3,293 soldiers sacrificed their lives, of which 179 were officers, 130 were junior commissioned officers and 2,984 were soldiers.

For martyrs, I can only say –

"Har Subah Ke Sath Aapko Yaad Karenge Aur Sadaiv Naman Karenge."

□

8
INDO-PAK WAR OF 1971

Agar koi vyakti kahta hai ki vo maut se nahi darta,
Ya to vo jhooth bol raha hai ya phir vo Gorkha hai.
(If anyone is saying that he is not afraid of death,
either he is lying or he is a Gorkha.)

The war of 1971 in a way was the result of Pakistan's harassment and oppression of its own people residing in its Eastern part which was known as East Pakistan those days. In the beginning of the year 1971, atrocities committed by Pakistani Government and soldiers on the inhabitants of its eastern part increased to the unbearable proportions, thus causing acute distress to Bangla-speaking majority who stared to migrate to India to escape from the inhuman conditions of living in the erstwhile East Pakistan. Migration of large population started affecting economy as well as demography of our states, like West Bengal, Manipur, Assam, and other North-Eastern States. Chief Ministers of those States had approached the Prime Minister time and again to resolve the issue by adopting effective remedial measures. Though government was making arrangements for their stay and food, yet the exodus of 10 lakh immigrants was a matter of serious concern. On 3rd March, 1971, curfew was imposed in Dhaka and Lt. General of Pakistan Army Tikka Khan was appointed as Marshal Law Administrator. It is said that Tikka Khan inflicted another Jallianwala Bagh-like massacre there – and he was called 'Butcher of Dhaka' as Pakistani Army started killing of innocent people at large and intellectuals specifically were picked up and killed in cold blood.

Field Marshal Sam Manekshaw

In India, at that time, Army Chief was Gen. Manekshaw, who was amongst the best of Army Officers. He was called by the then PM Indira Gandhi and told to move into East Pakistan and attack the Pakistani Army to help liberate the people of East Pakistan. Manekshaw told her that it would not be appropriate at that time to attack. Indira ji was not expecting such a reply and taunted him by saying what type of General he was to have refused to fight. General Sahib retorted that he is that type of General who fights to win big and not to lose. Madam Gandhi approved of General's plan when it was explained to her that the rainy season was about to approach, all their rivers will be flooded and even the fields would become soggy, restricting the swift movement of Indian troops and would severely affect soldiers' fighting abilities. Indira ji then asked, "So, when can we undertake the mission." Manekshaw replied that the month of November would be suitable for the attack. Indira ji agreed for that. Army started preparations with full vigour and astute planning. In the meanwhile, Mukti Vahini (Liberation Force), a gorilla warfare unit of predominantly Bengali militia under the leadership of Muzibur Rahman started a military rebellion against the Pakistani Army in East Pakistan. Pakistani leaders had the intension to enforce their culture on the people of East Pakistan. They wanted Urdu to be the main language by replacing of the native Bangla (Bengali) language. This was not at all acceptable to Bengali majority and became the bone of contention between them, leading to confrontation. Pakistani Army's atrocities were rising exponentially and so was the defiance by the native Bengalis. On 3rd December, 1971, Pakistani Air Force attacked many Air Bases of India, prominent among them were – Agra, Srinagar, Avantipur, Uttarlai, Jodhpur and Ambala.

This time around, unlike 1965, India was well prepared in advance. Indian forces initiated our own all-out attack on them. In fact, this war was thrust upon us blaming Indian forces assisting Mukti Bahini in military revolt, but the reality was that Pakistan could not manage the internal clashes and unrest in East Pakistan. The reason for internal clashes was the massive support of public to Muzibur Rahman's party in East Pakistan. This was not liked by Pakistan. When Pakistan attacked us, Indian Army retaliated with full force, resulting in full-fledged war.

This was one war in which we were required to secure our boundaries on Eastern side as well Western side. Our soldiers were full of enthusiasm and Indira ji had taken a decision to make East Pakistan a free country. On a broadcast from All India Radio, she said to the public that this war is imposed on us and we will fight it out. Entire country stood solidly behind her in support and even the leader of opposition, Shri Atal Bihari Vajpayee had pledged full support to the government. Not only this, after winning the war, Atal ji praised Indira Gandhi for her bold actions.

Undoubtedly, the one force which is headed by Manekshaw would certainly have great inspiration and high morale. Sam's full name was Sam Hormasji Jamshedji Manekshaw. He was born in a Parsi family on 3rd April, 1914 at Amritsar. His father was a Doctor by profession and had settled at Amritsar in 1900. All his children could speak fluent English, Hindi, Gujarati, and Punjabi languages.

Sam wanted to pursue Medicine study and wanted to go to foreign like his other brothers, but destiny had something else in store for him. He appeared for Army's selection examination and was selected in the first batch of Indian Military Academy Dehradoon. Later, Sam was sent to Burma for fighting against Japanese. There, Japanese had fired seven bullets at him in stomach, kidney, and liver. He was grievously injured. Seeing his gallantry, Commanding Officer hanged Military Cross on his chest in the warfield itself. It was the highest award of those pre-independence days. Sam's Commanding Officer did this because at that time, the award was not meant to be given to martyrs. Medical Officer of Regiment sent him to hospital at Pegue. There the Russian doctors initially declined to treat him as his injuries were critical and chances of survival were very slim. Sam's orderly Sher Singh pleaded with the doctors to attend him and forced them to start the treatment through determined persuation. Doctors were also surprised to see that despite being badly wounded for more than 36 hours, he could regain consciousness. Doctor asked Sam as to what has happened to him. The great warrior replied wittingly, "Kicked in stomach by an ass." Doctors liked his humorous response even on the face of death and surgeries were initiated. Through numerous operations and removal of bruised parts of intestine, he was saved. Thus, he was bestowed with a fresh lease of life so early in his military career. Sher Singh's unflinching pursuation and loyal efforts helped immensely in saving him. In the year 1961, the then Defence Minister V.K. Krishna Menon did not share cordial relations with Army Chief and his senior officers. As the first step towards the series of contemplated action against army tops brass, he had planned to teach a lesson to Manekshaw. At that time, Manekshaw was posted as Commandant at Wellingdon College, Nilgiri. Menon had constituted an inquiry committee against him and contemplated to conduct court martial. Chinese invaded India before these proceedings could commence in the year 1962, subsequent to the war. Menon had to forfeit his ministry. Later on, in an interview, Manekshaw jokingly mentioned that the Chinese came to save him. Just ponder over that if an efficient officer like Sam Bahadur was removed to serve somebody's grudge, our country would have suffered a great loss. Any way, after climbing the career staircase step by step, Sam went on to become Chief of Army Staff in the year 1969. After leading the army to the comprehensive victory in 1971 War, he was awarded with the second highest civilian award, Padma Vibhushan and was later made the first Field Marshal of Indian Army in 1973. Sam chose to spend rest of his retired life peacefully at Kunnur in Nilgiri Hills. The place had attracted his fancy as he had served many years at Nilgiri and had developed bond of affection and appreciation with it. One of the most luminous war heroes, the great Sam Bahadur passed away at the age of 94 years on 27th June, 2007. His prominently big statue has been placed at the entrance of Army College, Wellingdon. In January 2016, I got an opportunity to see that statue.

During the course of 1971 war, in order to divert attention of Indian Army from the eastern frontier of East Pakistan, where they were losing badly, Pakistani Army mobilised their full artillery might towards a post named Longewala located near Jaisalmer on western border. This was a design, meant to be a master-stroke of Pakistan, as India has deployed most of its forces at East Pakistan border, (nowadays Bangladesh). From 4th to 7th December, 1971, Pakistan had been attacking on this western front, which was effectively countered by Indian Army. At Longewala Sector, at the time of fierce attack from enemy, only 120 soldiers were deployed and Pakistan had attacked using force comprising 2,000 soldiers along with mechanised support of 65 Chinese T-59 Tanks. Though Pakistan enjoyed huge numerical and technological advantage, Indian soldiers made up for this through their abundant courage and determination. Major Kuldip Singh Chandpuri of Punjab Regiment was posted as the commander at Longewala and Lt. Dharamveer was posted at advance party location at Sadewala, 17 kms away from Longewala. Pakistanis

Major Kuldeep Singh Chandpuri

attacked the post in the night as they knew that Indian forces would not be able to provide aerial assistance to the troops by fighter bomber aircraft as the aircraft possessed by the nearby bases did not have night-combat abilities those days. Thus, it became imperative for the small number of infantry soldiers to engage the huge onslaught for the entire night till next morning and no way lose the post. If Kuldip Singh Chandpuri, Lt. Dharamveer, and their troops could not have stopped the evil designs of Pakistanis, they could have possibly reached Jaisalmer Airfield and the Indian Air Force might have been prevented from performing heroic feats which they had eventually achieved next morning. You can imagine the greatness of work they had done by thwarting the attack for the entire night. Border Security Force had also done a commendable job in the operation.

Major Kuldeeip Singh Chandpuri was awarded with Mahaveer Chakra for his able counter. Indian Air Force also did a commendable job next morning. The bomber sorties conducted by Sqadron Leaders Ravindra Nath Bali, M.S. Bawa, and Dilip Kumar Das and Flight Lieutenant Ramesh Chandra Gosain with able support from ground staff were very successful in defeating enemy force who was shocked in disbelief at the swift operations. In a few hours, Indian Air Force changed the complete scenario of battle in India's favour. Pakistan Army, that had boastfully planned to have their breakfast at Longewala, lunch at Ramgarh and dinner at Jaisalmer with the support of their 2,000 soldiers, received a severe jolt and had to beat a hasty retreat after having suffered great losses. All their dreams had

Barbed wire fencing separating India and Pakistan at Longewala

vanished in thin air. Pakistan had never anticipated that their mighty T-59 Tanks would be turned into mangle of metallic pieces by the air strike. A total of 34 tanks of Pakistani Army were destroyed by the superior skills displayed by the Indian Air Force peronnel. Major Kuldeep had played a vital role in this victory. The 23rd Punjab Regiment won many war accolades and was awarded with Yuddha Samman. Based on the story of Longewala battle, film producer J.P. Dutta had produced a feature film named "Border" in which real-life character of Major Kuldeep Chandpuri was enacted by Hindi film actor Sunny Deol. Major Chandpuri now resides at Chandigarh.

Here, if I do not mention about the Tanot Mata Temple, then the narration of this war would remain incomplete. Near the same border, a small temple of deity, popularly known as Tanot Mata is situated. The miraculous part of the incident was all the bombs and cells fired in the vicinity of Tanot Mata Temple had failed to explode. All such failed bombs have been put on display in this temple. It is generally believed by the BSF soldiers posted there that due to the blessings of Tanot Mata, the lives of the residents and soldiers were saved. This temple is managed by BSF personnel. In its premises, there is a guest house, where the guests of BSF can stay. I got that opportunity in the year 2012. We had stayed in the guest house overnight and had the fortune of participating in the first Arti (Prayer) conducted in the morning. The soldiers presently posted there had shown us those bombs which could not explode by the grace of Tanot Mata.

A Beautiful view of Longewala Border

After taking breakfast, we went to international border, which is only 12 kms away from the temple.

Entry of general public is prohibited in that sensitive area. Many a time, I have got opportunities to see India's boundary with neighbouring Pakistan and China – all sorts of borders, such as International Border / Line of Control / Line of Actual Control in which Cherrapunji, Leh, Kacch, Kargil, Chushul, Siachen, Firozpur, Khemkaran, Wagah, Bumla are prominent – but from Rajasthan's area, it was the first experience of seeing a border. After climbing on the watch tower, I could see the border through binoculars. I could spot some of the Pakistani soldiers moving around inside their area of control. Thereafter, we reached Longewala Sector and paid homage martyrs at their memorial. Pakistani Tanks (T-59) destroyed by India are kept on display there. We got ourselves photographed proudly atop those tanks. Who will not feel proud of our soldiers! The area was full of desert sand which could be horribly hot during the summer months. Another of my dreams of visiting that place of martyrs was fulfilled. After spending some quality time, we went back to Jaisalmer.

Author at Longewala Border

In the 1971 War, in the plains of J&K adjacent to Basantar River, another young and brave man, aged just 21 years, upheld the prestige and the name of our Tricolour. This young officer was none other than the famous son of our soil, Second Lieutenant Arun Khetrapal. He was commissioned in the Indian Army, following the footsteps of his illustrious father and grandfather, barely six months ago. This officer although was very young and inexperienced, yet had possessed great deal of courage and bravery that could have matched with any hardened war hero. He was hero of Basantar War, which is also known as war of Bada Pind amongst Pakistani army circles. Arun Khetrapal was born in Pune on 14th October, 1950. It was a sheer coincidence that after commissioning, he was posted in 17 Poona Horse. He received his elementary education in Lawrence School in Sanawar (Himanchal Pradesh). The security of Basantar area was strategically very vital for Arun, as roads of Jammu and Punjab merged there. He had displayed great combat skills maneuvering his tank. Arun destroyed four tanks of enemy. Suddenly, a bomb hit his tank – which resulted in fire. When Commanding Officer called Arun to retreat, he replied, "Still my gun is blazing and till such time it works, I will fight". Because of serious injuries incurred in the battle, he passed away, valiantly rendering service to the action till the last breath. Arun, a resident of Greater Kailash in Delhi, was honoured with the highest gallantry award Param Veer Chakra. In this battlefield, Poona Horse from Indian side and Lancers Regiment from Pakistani side were pitted against each other as dreaded enemies. Ironically, both these regiments were parts of Integrated Bombay Cavalry during the pre-independence era.

Second Lieutenant Arun Khetarpal

On 29th June 2016, I got to meet family of martyr Captain Vijayant Thapar, a war hero of Kargil War. On the same day, in the year 1999, the Captain had sacrificed his life while fighting very bravely at Kargil. Colonel (Retd.) V.N. Thapar, illustrious father of Captain Vijayant, had informed me that his son Vijayant used to idolise Arun Khetrapal as his hero and had visited his house in Greater Kailash many times. Strange are the ways of destiny. Vijayant had also attained martyrdom like his idol at the age of 22 years, after six months of commissioning in the Army. The grandfathers and fathers of both Arun and Vijayant were also in the Army. Such similarities in lives of these two greats are unique coincidences.

Flight Lieutenant Nirmaljit Singh Sekhon

Indian Air Force till now has received only one Param Veer Chakra and its only recipient is Flight Lieutenant Nirmal Jeet Singh Sekhon. He was born at Ludhiana on 17th July, 1945. His father had also served in the Indian Air Force. Flying aeroplanes was his childhood passion and he wanted to chase his dream since then. Sekhon realised his passion and became Fighter Pilot with Air Force. In 1971 War, he was posted at Srinagar Airbase. Pakistan had planned to attack the airbase. It had also planned to fly low till they reach Poonch to avoid being detected on any Indian Radar and then pull up to the altitude of 16,000 feet to attack Srinagar airbase. They knew even if their aircraft were to be detected by any radar, the flying time of only six minutes from there to the airfield would not allow enough time for IAF to regroup and plan any interception. Following this plan immaculately, their six sabre jets attacked Srinagar Airbase. The Pakistanis had partially succeed in their plan as Indian radars could not spot them. Indian air space was under dire threats and needed some 'do or die' attempts to save the base.

These hostile six of the much advanced sabre jets were flying over the air base and bombing. The young officer took off amidst the ongoing raid on his small and comparatively less advanced Gnat aircraft (later known as Ajeet-one that

Inner View of Air Force Museum, Palam, Delhi

cannot be conquered) and engaged them in fierce dog-fight, targeting to engage them one by one. This created complete chaos in enemy's camp as they could not have anticipated the stubborn resistance offered. Two enemy planes were destroyed by amazing fighting skills displayed by Sekhon. The other four sabre jets regrouped and attacked his plane simultaneously causing fire in the plane. He tried to bail himself out through ejection from the burning plane but unfortunately could not survive. Posthumously, he was honoured with Param Veer Chakra Award. Air Force Museum at Palam in Delhi is a place worth seeing. Here, the plane flown by Nirmaljeet Singh Sekhon is displayed. We had bowed our heads with respect in front of the statue of Sekhon placed there. They have built a war memorial in the premises of the museum. This is a unique museum in the entire India where different articles and memorabilia used in IAF from its inception (1932) till now have been put on display. The display includes the uniforms donned by IAF men down the years, many historical photographs, weapon systems, information about martyrs and, most importantly, those aircraft which were used during First and Second World Wars, Indo-Pak Wars of 1971 and 1999 including vintage Douglas Knot, Canberra, and MIGs. Much debris, broken

Author at Airforce War Memorial, Palam

parts of Pakistani planes destroyed by our bravehearts has also been displayed there. We were greatly satisfied after paying homage to martyrs here.

Author and his spouse in front of Canberra Aircraft at Air Force Museum, Palam

Back home in Delhi, we have India Gate, the most popular War Memorial of our country. It is located in the heart of New Delhi on the Rajpath. India Gate is a forty-three metres high beautiful architectural structure, constructed, as a memorial for 10,000 soldiers who had laid down their lives during the First World War and the Afghan conflict, in the year 1931, using Red and Pink Stones. Names of all 13,300 martyrs including the Officers of British Army have been inscribed on this magnificent monument. Its magnificent architecture drew inspiration from the world-famous memorial "Arc de Triomphe" located in Paris. The British architect of New Delhi, Mr. Edwin Lutyens had designed India Gate

World Famous War Memorial India Gate, Delhi

In the memory of dead and unknown soldiers who attained martyrdom in 1971

Indo-Pak War, a memorial known as Amar Jawan Jyoti (Flame of Immortal Soldier) has been constructed under the India Gate, where the flame keeps on glowing continuously. As a token to commemorate the unknown martyr, a gun in the reverse position has been placed on a pedestal with a helmet of an unknown soldier on its top. As an annual ritual, Indian Prime Minister, Defence Minister along with the Chiefs of Army, Navy, and Air Force staff visit the Amar Jawan Jyoti to pay their homage to the unknown soldiers by placing a wreath every year on 26th January. When India Gate was built, statue of King George V adorned the place, the statue was later shifted to Coronation Park in the year 1968. The surroundings of India Gate are well known for their greenery with lush green lawns and big trees all around. Thousands of people visit this place and throng it till late at night, a happening hangout location for Delhiites and tourists too. Such is the attraction that anybody coming to Delhi likes to see India Gate.

For the last few years, there have been talks in the government parlance about making a National War Memorial, especially to commemorate sacrifices of Indian soldiers. At last, Modi Government has decided to realise the dream by initiating construction of war memorial at Princess Park near India Gate, where presently government officials reside.

Major Hoshiar Singh

Another great warrior of 1971 War was – Major Hoshiar Singh, he was born in Sonepat, Haryana on 5th May, 1936. He was posted at Shakargarh Sector during the war. Pakistani Forces attacked his post thrice between 15th and 17th December, 1971, but the valiant troops ably led by Major Hoshiar Singh foiled their attacks, forcing Pakistan to beat hasty retreat. Major kept morale of every soldier very high by continuous encouragements and through personal display of bravery. He led from the front and, in the ensuing fierce battle, suffered serious injuries, but didn't consider to withdraw himself and the troop supported him to continue the fight. They left the advanced field only after the declaration of ceasefire. He was awarded with Param Veer Chakra for the display of exemplary courage, leadership and bravery. Major Hoshiar Singh had fought both 1965 and 1971 Wars. He had retired after becoming Brigadier and later left for heavenly abode on 6th December, 1998.

Lance Naik Albert Ekka

Another great warrior of this war, Lance Nayak Albert Ekka was also awarded with Param Veer Chakra for gallantry. His posting was at Ganga Sagar (West Bengal) area. He was one of the finest players of Hockey. Originally native of Gumla in Jharkhand, he was a warrior par excellence.

The 1971 War was one such war where all the three arms of military services, viz. Indian Army, Indian Navy, and Indian Air Force played significant role to the perfection. After having described the efficient contributions from the Army and Air Force, let us now talk about the important contribution made by Indian Navy. During 1971 War, Chief of Navy, Admiral Nanda had met Indira Gandhi with a request to accord Navy with full freedom to plan strategic maritime warfare against the enemy. Indira ji permitted them with the freedom to go ahead. Admiral Nanda had devised a unique maritime strategy and launched all-out attack on the Pakistan Navy, which resulted into immense monetary loss of millions but more significantly finished one-third of its naval strength. India very well knew that if Karachi Port was destroyed, Pakistan Navy will not be able to move towards East Pakistan to extend its support. Through adopting an astute strategic offensive 'Operation Trident', Admiral Nanda and his brave officers managed to put Oil Tankers parked at Karachi Port on fire in addition to the complete distruction of their warships. Small ships equipped with deadly missiles were sent on a mission towards Karachi from the Mumbai and Kutch ports. With a view to avoid refuelling problem en route, these small ships were towed with the help of bigger ships. The interesting part of the mission was that with the aim of keeping the strategy a top secret affair, Indian Naval Officers talked in Russian language (they could do so as they were recently trained in Russia) – Pakistanis could not understand a word of their conversation and were caught unawares of the developments. In the first surprise attack, they thought that it was an air raid from Indian Air Force, but by the time they could realise what stuck them, the complete demolition was inflicted. PNS Ghazi was also destroyed to Indian Navy Vishakapatnam which of proved fatal for Pakistan Navy.

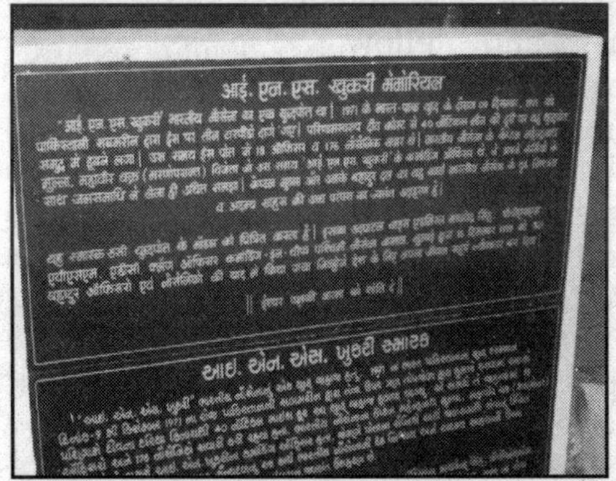

A Stone describing the history of Khukri War Memorial in Diu

One amongst these ravaging Frigate Ships was INS Khukhri, commanded by Captain Mahendra Nath Mulla. The very daring and highly determined Naval war hero,

Captain Mahendra Nath Mulla

Captain Mulla was born in Allahabad on 15th May, 1926.INS Khukhri was a black wood class submarine destroyer frigate that was manufactured in England in the year 1950. It was deployed at the Naval base of Diu. While engaging with enemy submarines on the night of 9th December, 1971, it was stuck with multiple torpedoes fired by an enemy submarine causing massive fire to the ship. Subsequently, Captain instructed his sailors and fellow officers to evacuate from the sinking ship to safety but the massive damage coupled with fire took a very heavy toll by snatching lives of 176 Navy sailors and 18 officers. It is said that when the ship was sinking, Captain Mulla stood peacefully on the deck smoking a cigarette fearlessly. He could display such courage in the face of certain death just because he had made up his mind that in pursuit to save fellowmen, he would lay down his life observing the highest tradition of Navy where the captain doesn't abandon his ship but sacrifices his life along with the sinking ship if all others could not be evacuated. Thus, he chose to make the supreme sacrifice. He was posthumously awarded Mahaveer Chakra for his bravery. Whereas, on one hand, Navy was celebrating glorious victory of Karachi, on the other hand, they were grieving the death of fellow 194 brave souls. After

Khukri War Memorial at Diu

1947, this was the first instance where our warship was affected by enemy's torpedo. A memorial has been raised to commemorate the sacrifices of these immortal martyrs. I had been fortunate to have offered my homage to these gallant martyrs.

In this war, Indian forces brought enemy forces on their knees by delivering decisive and crushing blows within merely 13 days between 3rd and 16th December. After conceding ignominious defeat, Pakistan's Lt. General A.A.K. Niyazi surrendered to Lt. General Jagjit Singh Arora of Indian Army and in that unprecedented surrender, 93,000 Pakistani soldiers laid their weapons at Race Course Area of

Pakistan's Lt. General Niyazi Signing the instrument of surrender before Lt. General Jagjit Singh Aurora, Maj Gen JFR Jacob is standing behind Niyazi.

Dhaka in complete surrender. This crushing loss and abject surrender proved to be the greatest shame in the history of Pakistan and is the most glorious feat for India. We can not forget to mention the man who achieved this lone case of Public Surrender in the world, his name was Maj Gen JFR Jacob. He was a Jewish Indian Army officer born in Calcutta. He coned Niyazi to surrender to India. JFR Jacob also fought in World War-II & 1965 war. After retirement he served as Governor of Goa & Punjab. In New Delhi, in Dec. 2016, he left for heavenly abode. General Manekshaw and Indian forces had added a glorious chapter in realms of Indian history. Indira Gandhi had displayed an astute iron-like will to the world and declared to the world through

General (Later Field Marshall) Sam Manekshaw after the victory in 1971 war with proud Countrymen

radio broadcast from All India Radio that new country named Bangladesh has born. At last, spirations for freedom of Bangladeshi people had won and Mukti Vahini achieved its desired goal but in the struggle, it lost lives of about 10 lakh Bangladeshi people and also rendered about a crore of Bangladeshis refugees in India.

During this war, about 2,500 soldiers attained martyrdom and 94,000 Pakistani soldiers were taken as Prisoners of War. Despite the huge victory in the battlefield, where 94,000 POW were taken by Military, it could not yield the desired result for India on the negotiation table during the consequent Shimla Accord. The overwhelming advantage that India enjoyed that time could have been put to great use through deft negotiations on resolving the nagging issues such as Kashmir, Siachen, etc. Therefore, our intellectuals and war experts still opine that we won 1971 War on the field but had lost it on the negotiation table.

□

9

SIACHEN : PRIDE OF OUR NATION

Live Peacefully At Your Home, Indian Army Is Deployed At Front For Safety.
— Indian Army

It was an evening in July 2016 when I was enjoying a hot cup of tea with Lt. Col. Shashikant Sharma at his residence in Barrackpur. He informed me that he had been posted at Siachen twice in the past. Hearing this, I was enthralled and asked him, "Sharma ji – for many years, I am nursing a desire to see Siachen – can I go there?" He said, "Yes, you can go there but upto Siachen base camp only, as beyond that point, it is a very difficult route and for travelling further, a special training is required and also would need a special permission from the Indian Army." Hearing all this, I started visualising that someday I would be able to go there. Sharmaji provided me with other requisite information also – which were very helpful.

I was not expecting that God will listen to my prayer so quickly and grant me an opportunity so early. After two months, i.e. in September 2016, I went to Siachen – known as Mecca for tourists. Siachen was discovered by a British citizen Henry Starchi. When I reached Siachen Base Camp, I was quite amazed that was it really me to have put my feet in the sacred place of greatest sacrifices by our valiant soldiers. But the fact was that my long-cherished dream had turned into reality. On 25th September, 2016, we had landed in Leh at 7 o'clock in the morning by flight from Delhi. We

Entrance Gate of Hall of Fame located at Leh

decided to take rest in order to acclimatise our bodies with the weather and the high altitude of Leh till 4 o'clock in the evening and then venture out to pay our homage to martyrs at the War Memorial. Last time, when I had visited Leh in 2007, the Memorial used to be small, but this time around, I found it to be a bigger one with some new sections which consist of very useful and meaningful information about our gallant acts during Leh and Kargil War and also displays weaponries seized from the enemy forces. Vital information about Param Veer Chakra and Mahaveer Chakra Awardees is also given here. Hall of Fame was built in 1986 and in June 2016, a major portion of it was opened for public. This place is divided into – Yuddha Smarak, Yuddha Sangrahalaya, and Shaurya Sthal (here Smareeka of martyrs is kept). Recently, the Hall of Fame is selected as the best museum. It is one amongst the best 25 museums of Asia.

Every evening, National Tricolour is lowered down here – a small contingent of Army lowers it down by paying regards to martyrs and next day in the morning, it is raised again with regards. After seeing this for about 15 minutes,

War Memorial Situated at Leh

a documentary film was shown regarding Kargil War. The film is very heart-touching and moving. It shows gallantry of our jawans, whc defeated the enemy in a befitting manner. There is a counter run by Army where you can get to buy souvenir (*Smareeka*) and many other attractive articles. From here, I purchased a woolen cap for my father at a very reasonable price.

After about a week, before my visit to Leh, Pakistani terrorists had attacked Army Camp at Uri and killed 18 of our jawans. Because of that, there was tension in border. We were not sure whether permission to visit base camp will be given to us or not? While having dinner, we decided that if permission was not

Author at World's Highest Motorable Road, Khardungla Pass

granted, we would stay at Nubra. Next day in the morning, albeit a bit delayed, we got the much-awaited permission for proceeding to Siachen Base Camp. We were very happy with the prospects of the visit and commenced our travel by road. On the way to Siachen, we passed by Khardungla Pass, world's highest road at a staggering height of 18,380 feet and managed to reach Army Traffic Control Post (TCP) located at Sasoma by 5.30 in the evening. On the way, the scenic beauty of Shyok River provided magnificent view. From Sasoma one has to travel 40 more kilometres to reach Siachen Base Camp on a road that was patchy with certain good stretches and also several bad stretches. Because of the late-receipt of permission, we were getting delayed in reaching the Base Camp. The Nubra River originates from Siachen Glacier and while flowing ahead Nubra River merges with Shyok River before finally merging into the piece Indus River at Skardu Sindhu or Indus which is an important river of Pakistan with total length of 3,100 kms. Sindhu River flowing in India is not very big and one can see it to be quite narrow at some places in Leh. I was also surprised as to how Sindhu becomes so big in Pakistan as to become its lifeline. Later on, I could understand that it is because of its merger with Shyok and Numbra might have contributed significantly.

Siachen War Memorial

Indus originates from Kailash Mansarovar and through Ladakh, it enters India and before Baltistan, it enters into Pakistan. One after another, many rivers like Jhelum, Chenab, Ravi, Sutlej, and Beas merge into Sindhu and at last, it merges into Arabian sea near Karachi. A stream from here used to go to Kot Lakhpat in the Kutch area. Luckily, I got an opportunity to visit from origin of Indus upto its last point. Five percent of Sindhu is in India, 3 percent is in Tibet and 92 percent is in Pakistan. On the banks of Sindhu River, 'Hindu' word was originated and from Hindu, Hindustan was named.

Finally, in the evening, at about 6.20, we reached Siachen base camp and paid homage to martyrs at Siachen War Memorial. In December 2015, Defence Minister had informed Lok Sabha that since 1984 till then, 869 soldiers had lost their lives at Siachen. Unfortunately, most of them had died due to severely inclement weather that can freeze blood. In February 2016, owing to an avalanche and snow storm, we lost our 10 soldiers. At Siachen, a memorial of an

Author at Siachen war Memorial

unknown soldier is displayed by placing gun in reverse position with a helmet hanging on that. Siachen Base Camp is located at a height of 13,000 feet, whereas the posts made at glaciers are located even higher with the maximum height of 21,000 feet. Here, in this region, there are about 160 posts of Indian Army. On these posts along with soldiers, officers are also posted. Pakistan is only 13 km away from Siachen base camp. Therefore, we have stationed our artilleries on the bank of Nubra River.

Now, I will let you know about the history and geography of Siachen. Fully white Siachen Glacier comes out of Karakoram range of Himalayas. This glacier is 76.4 kilometres long and the entire area is spread in about 5,000 sq. kilometres. Here, temperature goes 70 degree below zero. This place is also known as Third Pole. As you are aware that other two poles are – North Pole and South Pole.

All soldiers and officers are required to walk upto their post. Helicopter is used for supplying food and military aid to the higher areas. Before posting here, soldiers are required to undergo a very hard and strenuous high-altitude warfare training. On successful completion of the training, they are deployed at the Siachen for a period of three months. Here in Siachen, Battle School is also there. Aspiring mountaineer of Everest expedition are also trained here. Since the last few years, Army has been offering opportunity to general public to track on the glacier. Nominations are invited through notices on newspapers. Health and experience are the main criteria for selection. Army's Northern Command supervises these activities. It is definitely a great step in adventure planning. General public should also know that under what grave situation soldiers are protecting the country.

As I have intimated earlier, officers and soldiers are required to walk upto their respective posts from Siachen Base Camp. It takes about 21 days of walk in certain cases. In the west of Siachen, a mountain range named Saltoro is located, which segregates the Nubra Valley of Baltistan and

Ladakh. In the Balti language, the word 'Siachen' means 'a place where roses are found in abundance'.

After meeting with Base Commander, it became quite dark and we were required to reach Sumur, which was 80 kms from Base Camp. Col. Saheb asked us to go cautiously, keeping vigil on the road as sometimes water level of Nubra suddenly rises, making travelling difficult. In this area, one phrase is very popular *"yah jagah itni banjar aur iske daria itne unche hain ki yaha sabse gahre dost aur sabse gahre dushman hi aate hain"*. Here, it is a challenge to pass every minute; at this highest place our soldiers perform so very well – their dedication is commendable.

Here, for obtaining drinking water, the ice is required to be melted first and chlorine is added to it to make it fit for human consumption. During the posting here, soldiers experience difficulty in having sound sleep, memory becomes weak, weight starts reducing and problems like acute mountain sickness is very common. Despite so many odds and difficulties, every officer and soldier dreams to get a posting at Siachen at least once. We bow down before their determination.

After 1947-48 War between India and Pakistan, an agreement was reached to in the year 1949 regarding Boundary Line in which Ceasefire Line was demarcated. The agreement contained an error – the last point before Siachen Glacier was shown as NJ 9842 but the area after Siachen was not clearly demarcated and it was just mentioned 'beyond the glacier in the north' and this became the cause for dispute.

In the Shimla Agreement of 1972, ceasefire line was renamed as Line of Control. At that time, we had a golden opportunity for getting the above mistake corrected by clear demarcation, but we did not press for it as it was believed that the then PM of Pakistan had persuaded our PM Indiraji to resolve this issue on a later date, which never arrived.

In 1980, Pakistan, in the name of trekking, started its nefarious activities here. By 1982-83, it was clear that the

Subedar Bana Singh

motives of Pakistan were not fair. Up to 1984, Pakistan had created posts on Saltaro Hills and occupied the same. It was revealed that Pakistan may take possession of many other places. Upon receipt of this information, Indian Army became active and with the assistance of Air Force, started Operation 'Meghdoot' and Pakistani soldiers were pushed back. Indian Army first took control over Bilaphond La and Sia La. In this operation, "Cheetah" helicopter played a great role. At that time, this was the only helicopter which could fly at the altitude of 18,000 feet. On 14th April, 1984, Indian Army pushed back Pakistani Army from Saltaro and made such posts at places from where Pakistan could not see the Siachen once again. In this operation, Subedar Bana Singh had displayed exemplary courage far beyond the call of duty. For his exceptional bravery, he was awarded with Param Veer Chakra, the highest gallantry award of India. In addition to this award, a hilltop has been named after him as 'Bana Top'. I am fortunate that I got a chance to meet Capt. Bana Singh ji in person in January 2017, when he came to Delhi to attend Republic day parade. Along with him I also got to meet Rifleman Sanjay Singh ji & Subedar Yogendra Singh Yadav. Presently, these three are the living Param Veer Chakra awardees.

From 1984, we started deploying our force in this Ocean of Ice. Though, as per an estimate, our per day expenditure at Siachen is six crores and it is a point of debate whether such huge daily expenditure is appropriately justified. In my view, this expenditure towards safeguarding of nation is appropriate and necessary because Pakistan cannot be relied upon. When would they betray is not known. Another reason in justification is the Chinese boundary is also not very far. Area near Baltistan is under control of China and in view of the close relations between China and Pakistan, these days we cannot leave this area unattended. We should not forget that one reason of Kargil War was trying to annex possession of Siachen.

It is said that 1999 Kargil War was designed by Parvez Musharraf because he was posted in Siachen in 1980 and had to suffer the great ignomious defeat of forced expulsion of Pakistani Army. Suffering from such shock, he designed Kargil War. Once when a press reporter had asked Musharraf why Pakistan did Kargil, he replied why India did Siachen? This utterance silently answers many questions. By now, we had a number of rounds of peace talks about Siachen – the last was on 23rd November, 2003 – wherein it was decided to adhere to complete ceasefire and since then, the situation is peaceful there.

Interior view of O.P. Baba Mandir Located at Siachen Base Camp

In the Base Camp area, there is one O.P. Baba Mandir (Om Prakash Baba). Every soldier, before proceeding for glacier, prays here and takes his blessings. O.P. Baba was posted in Army and it is said that his soul still exists there and he protects soldiers from all difficulties. In our Army area, this is the third such temple which I came across. On the way to Tawang at Jaswant Garh, I had seen similar a temple of Jaswant Singh ji and on the way to Nathula, we could see another such temple of Harbhajan Baba. Both two were Indian Army are when a time. It is a common belief amongst soldiers that these souls of martyrs protect them from all the danger lurking around.

Siachen post was visited many a time by Shri George Fernandes, former Defence Minister. He was involved in solving probems of soldiers very meticulously. He used to get annoyed at any inordinate delay in procurement of logistics required for Siachen due to bureaucratic hurdles and at one point of time, he had advised Defence Secretary to visit the place to experience the tough living conditions there. Thereafter, all the requirements of Army were met well in time.

In June 2005, Shri Manmohan Singh became the first Prime Minister to visit Siachen. The then Army Chief J. J. Singh received him. Dr. A.P.J. Abdul Kalam was the first President to visit Siachen. Sh. Narendra Modi also visited the place after becoming Prime Minister.

After enjoying hot tea and the deliberations with Base Commander, we took leave and proceeded to our destination – Sumur. Visiting Siachen base has become my life time achievement. At 10.30 p.m. we reached our destination – Sumur. The purpose of an visit was fulfilled.

□

10
KARGIL WAR, 1999

"Main Tiranga Faharakar Wapas Aaunga; ya Tirange me Lipatkar Aaunga, Lekin mai Vapas Avashya Aaunga".

"Either I will come back after hoisting the Tricolour (Indian flag), or I will come back wrapped in it, but I will be back for sure."

– Capt. Vikram Batra

India and Pakistan has till now fought total four wars in the years 1947, 1965, 1971, and 1999 and Pakistan suffered huge defeats in all of its misadventures. Pakistan crossed limits of all decency when India's Prime Minister had visited Lahore in the year 1999 for a Peace Talk as a step to further goodwill with the perennially hostile nation but Pakistan under the garb of peace talks was conspiring to commit an unparalleled act of betrayal by deceitfully planning an offensive against India at the same time. As a part of mute agreement, military forces of both the sides used to withdraw their soldiers from the advance positions in the hilly areas of Kargil, Dras, Batalik during winter months and this mutual understanding continued without any problem till May 1999. The trouble was initially spotted by Tashi Namgyal a local shepherd belonging to the Buddhist faith, who had observed some heavily armed people who had infiltrated into Indian Territory. He informed about this activity to the Indian Army immediately. Army then sent a search party to patrol the area under the leadership

Captain Saurabh Kalia

of Captain Saurabh Kalia. The search party could not return alive. Their severely mutilated bodies with tell tale signs of gory brutality all over them. This inhuman act caused very deep anguish and anger not only amongst the army ranks but also amongst the whole of India. It has now become clear that Pakistan troops in garb of terrorists had wrongfully infiltrated into our side of LOC and taken unauthorised possession of that area. It is believed that Pakistan took control of our 130 posts spread over in area of 132 sq. k.m. (which used to be vacated in the winter-extreme cold). Now, we may attribute this lapse to the failure of our intelligence or whatever else, the only recourse left to our forces was not only to challenge the enemy who was sitting atop those hills in a strategically advantageous position but also to force them to retreat and regain every inch of our motherland. Pakistan's actual intention was to capture National Highway between Leh and Srinagar so that Siachen and Leh can be conquered. They had this dream in their hearts during the past conflicts in 1947, 1965 and 1971.

Kargil War officially went on for two months and was declared as concluded on 26th July, 1999. At that time, I was 24 years youth and these developments had made my blood to boil as much as that of any other true patriotic Indian. During those days, I had reached Jammu on 23rd July, 1999 when the war was to conclude three days henceforth, on way to Amarnath pilgrimage. By that time, all the area captured by Pakistan was regained by Indian Army by driving the enemy forces out. The main centre of war was located at a place known as Dras, which is 64 kms away from Kargil. Dras is located at the distance of only 48 kms from Baltal (Amarnath Base Camp) too. During that visit, some of my friends from our group went further ahead to see the actual war-ravaged condition of Dras but I could not make it then due to some reasons. But then and there, I took a vow to visit Dras and Kargil to pay my heartfelt homages to the martyrs, this dream was fulfilled in July 2007.

We had decided to visit Leh and places located around it on 5th July, 2007. In the meantime, we conducted extensive research and then finalised the itinerary. I had called my friend Shri Rajiv Badu, a resident of Jammu who was quite familiar with the routes and discussed the probable route for Srinagar from Leh. The route suggested by him and other options of making the tour memorable were further discussed with a serving Lt. General, a relative of my another friend Gaurav Pathak. The Lt. General generously made arrangements for our stay at Army Guest House at Leh. As another kind gesture, he also arranged for our stay at Kargil, the main centre of Indo-Pak War of 1999. I was feeling quite excited with the prospects of my visit to Kargil, Dras, Mushkoh Valley and pay my homage and respects our valiant soldiers who had laid down their lives.

At last, with the grace of God on 5th July, 2007, I along with my two friends Gaurav Pathak and Tarun ji, took, flight from Indira Gandhi International Airport for Leh. Duration of flight was 1.05 hours. Just after half-an-hour of our take-off, we could sense the excitement increased in the air within the flight as the aircraft was just about to start flying above the snow-clad mountains of Manali. The beauty offered by the picturesque view all around mesmerised each one of the passengers aboard. The scenic splendour was so captivating that some of the foreign tourists started screaming with joy. It was but natural that all the passengers were trying to capture the beauty by clicking photographs from all the best possible angles. The spread of natural beauty was so magnificent that everyone in the plane got fascinated with the wonderful experience. After having flown over the snow-clad beautiful mountains of Manali, when we got to see brown, naked hills full of rocky terrains underneath the

Kargil War Memorial at Dras

plane, we came to know that we were nearing towards Leh. Very soon thereafter, the aircraft landed at 6.35 hours in the morning at Bakula Rinpoche Airport which is the highest Civilian airport in the world. At the airport, two soldiers of Indian Army received us with a very warm welcome and we immediately proceeded for Army Guest House. Such a nice environment and atmosphere prevailing in Leh is perhaps very difficult to be found elsewhere in any other corner of India. The air was devoid of even a hint of pollution. All the nice things heard about Leh were turning to be absolutely true. After a drive of about 15 minutes, we reached Army Guest House which looked quite mundane from outside, but was very plush inside with many facilities such as dish antena, double bed, drawing room, kitchen and even a small library, etc., making us feel the ambiance as wonderful.

Since Leh is situated at a very good height of about 10,500 feet from sea Level, it is normally advisable to take 24 hours rest upon reaching there with a view to acclimatise oneself with that environment, otherwise some health issues might crop up.

After 2-3 hours of complete rest, we decided to go for local sightseeing in Leh. After 1962 War with China, a War Memorial has been raised there. We went to the memorial and paid our homage.

After staying for two days at Leh, we proceeded for Kargil and Dras. After two hours of arduous drive, we entered into the area of Batalik Sector. Batalik again was one of the main centres in 1999 Kargil War. The famous words of Captain Manoj Pandey, the war hero of Batalik,

Hero of Kargil War- Captain Manoj Kumar Pandey

originally from Lucknow, who was posthumously awarded with Param Veer Chakra for his valour and exceptional courage shown on the Zuber top, started ringing in our ears: *"Yadi apna shaurya siddh karne se purv, meri mrityu aa jae toh, ye meri kasam hai ki mrityu ko hi maar daloonga."* (If death comes before I have proved my valour, I swear to kill the death itself.) Then, we reached NH-1 where we saw a board displaying this message 'Beware, enemy is watching you'.Limbu, a soldier who was accompanying us, had told us about a Pakistani post, located just a little away, from where they could easily see us. Just with the mere thought of being within their line of visible sight ran a chill down our spines. We were thrilled. We took our photographs standing near the signage board. We could see a small spring of majestic green water flowing nearby. The water was very cold and tasted very sweet. I had not probably seen a more beautiful spring elsewhere so far. After one hour of further drive, we entered into Kargil. It was an emotional moment for me –because that was the place where hundreds of our soldiers had sacrificed their lives for protecting the honour of our country. We were accommodated in a cosy room in the guest house

Ashes Urn Kept at Kargil War Memorial, Dras

Board at the entrance of Kargil, cautioning vistors about " the Enemy is watching us"

of Gorkha Regiment. In the evening, we met the Commanding Officer of that post, Colonel Gehlot. Colonel was originally from Rajasthan and we found him to be quite jovial and lively human being. He sent his driver to show us the Kala Pahar Chowki in his vehicle. Kala Pahar Chowki is the last post of India and from there, Pakistan could be seen. It was a matter of happiness for us that even at that height, Satellite TV facilities were made available for recreation of our soldiers serving there. We cannot forget the exhilarating experience of relishing hot tea and *pakoras* while looking across the international border.

On-duty soldiers told me that every soldier greets each other by saying "Jai Mata Di". They told us that they greet in this manner because of presence of a small temple of "Mata Sherowali" on the hilltop. They further added that during 1971 War, when they had only 100 soldiers pitted against a comparatively larger strength of 500 Pakistani soldiers, the Mata appeared in their dreams and ordered them to retaliate through fierce return attack. Obeying the Goddess, Pakistanis were defeated comprehensively and enemies were made to retreat. Later on, it was divulged that Pakistanis were seeing thousands of Indian soldiers who, in fact, were 100 only. The top of the temple as well as the army post was adorned by a red-colour flag that has "Om" written on one side, whereas picture of Hanuman ji is displayed on another. When enquired, it was told that this flag is hoisted at every Army Post on the front. Indian soldiers normally are very God-fearing and have immense faith in gods and goddesses. After returning to the guest house, we became fresh after having bath. I can recollect that Hindi movie *Don-2* was being telecast on TV that day. I made our handycam and still cameras ready for next day's sojourn to one of the most important places of our tour Dras – from where the Kargil War had started.

Next day began very early for us at 5 AM in the morning. With an aim to enjoy the magnificent scenery and pleasant weather, we went for a morning walk. Our lungs experienced very refreshing air after Leh and we felt thoroughly rejuvenated. In the morning, after having our breakfast at about 8 am, we started our drive towards Dras. A Major was deputed to take us around the place. Packed lunch, four folding chairs, a small table, drinking water and few juice packs were kept in the vehicle. Just after travelling a little ahead, we could have a glimpse of Dras River. After some distance from here, Dras River enters into Pakistan. As weather was not very clear, it was quite cloudy. The heavy cloud cover was probably delaying visibility of Tiger Hill. First of all, we could see the place, from where our Army used to fire from Bofors Tanks during the Kargil War and media, was seen reporting. I silently offered my homage to Captain Vikram Batra. Captain Batra of Kashmir Rifles had displayed immense courage and his gallant and heroic actions on the warfield won the greatest military honour – Param Veer Chakra. He is still remembered for his very popular comment made during one of the interviews – wherein he had said after having accomplished a successful mission – *"Ye dil mange more"*(My heart longs for more). That interview which inspired millions of youth

Hero of Kargil War- Captain Vikram Batra

Hero of Kargil War- Captain Anuj Nayyar

was conducted at that place. Pakistani soldiers were afraid of him. While communicating amongst themselves, they used to refer to him as "Shershah" – King of Lions. His fearless approach was instrumental in driving out Pakistanis from our motherland. This brave officer laid his life in the successful mission of regaining an army post called 4875 top. Prior to this victory, he had conquered 5140 post on 20th June. That Top is now renamed after him as 'Batra Top'. After travelling for some more time, we entered into Mushkoh Valley. At this beautiful Valley, another braveheart Captain Anuj Nayyar of Jat Regiment had sacrificed his life. Before laying his life, he had managed to terminate nine Pakistani soldiers. He was awarded with Mahavir Chakra. In August 2017, I got to meet Mrs. Meena Nayyar mother of Captain Anuj Nayyar currently she is running a petrol pump near Mayur Vihar area of Delhi. Age wise Anuj was one week older then me, we also share a common zodiac sign i.e. virgo. I took blessings of Mrs. Nayyar & handed over a copy of hindi version of this book "Deshbhakti ke Paawan Teerth". Here, I feel it very necessary to mention about another great war hero, Major Vivek Gupta. He became a martyr while conquering Tolo Ling Post. Next day, when his body was brought to Delhi for cremation, his wife Dr. Rajshree Gupta who herself is an Army

A Beautiful View of Mushkoh Valley

Doctor Rajshree Gupta Paying tribute to her martyr Husband Major Vivek Gupta

officer paid regards in full uniform. At this emotional moment of great personal loss, it shows her courage, devotion to duty and dedication towards the nation. We salute her thousands of times for this act of exemplary bravery even in face of extreme adversity. Her photograph which was published in *India Today* is still afresh in my memory. In the initial stages of this war, Indian Army had suffered a lot due to insufficient knowledge of enemy prowess. Thereafter, General V.P. Malik, Chief of Army Staff changed the strategy and we started winning back all our posts rapidly.

In another inspiring act of valour, an young officer named Lieutenant Vijayant Thapar belonging to 2, Rajputana Rifles while undertaking final assault on the enemy in this war had written a letter to his parents mentioning, "By the time you get this letter, I will be observing you all from the sky enjoying hospitalities of the *Apsaras* in Heaven." Probably, he had the premonition that he would make supreme sacrifice for the cause of nation and would never return. Same thing

Hero of Kargil War- Lieutenant Vijayant Thapar

happened, the braveheart attained martyrdom. He further wrote two very important things in the same letter, the first one about he had no regrets whatsoever and, in fact, even if he were to become human again, he would join the Army again and fight for his nation. The second thing he mentioned

Mother and Father of Lt. Vijyant Thapar, Hero of Kargil War

was, "If you can, please come and see where the Indian Army fought for your tomorrow." Lt. Vijayant Thapar belonged to an illustrious family with tradition of serving nation with both his grandfather and father were in Army. A prominent road of NOIDA has been named as "Shaheed Vijayant Thapar Marg". It has to be our endeavour not to forget these sacrifices under any circumstances. This is the least that we can offer as an indebted nation. I would like to mention that every year as Kargil Vijay Diwas Colonel Thapar personally go to the place in Dras section when his son Vijayant Thapar had sacrificed his life for the nation.

In this war, Yogendra Singh Yadav and Rifleman Sanjay Singh were also awarded Param Veer Chakra for their gallantry in face of extreme challenging conditions. They are the living legends of Indian Army. Yogendra Singh, now a Subedar was only 19-year-old soldier during this war and, thus, is the youngest to receive Param Veer Chakra so far.

Subedar Yogendra Singh Yadav

Lunch was spread on folding dining table and chairs for us at the foot of the Tiger Hill. It was amazing to fathom as to how, at such difficult terrains, our soldiers would have climbed and defeated Pakistani Troops sitting on the top above. In fact, only our soldiers could have made this almost unachievable feat possible. This fact was also confirmed by Pentagon of America that only Indian soldiers could have accomplished that. After lunch, we went to see War Memorial at Dras. There in the museum, articles related with soldiers, arms and ammunitions, and weapon systems are exhibited.

Dras is one of the coldest places on the earth, where temperature falls below the bone chilling – 60°C. I just by the mere thought of how our soldiers could have fought and won during hostile peak winter on 9th January, 1995 against the hostile forces which occupied strategically higher locations. Kudos to the great force as our minds fill with great respect and sense of deep gratitude. At last, we could see Tiger Hill. It was strategically very vital to recapture that post as Pakistanis by sitting atop the post could have blocked National Highway No. 1 but for the timely regaining of control it could have possibly be dangerous for Siachen and Leh too. Indian Army once again had proved its worth by living upto its reputation of being

A Beautiful View of Tiger Hill

Dras, the second coldest inhabited place in the World overlooking Tiger Hill

one of the best in the world. After paying homage to martyrs at the memorial, we proceeded for Kargil. In this war, another hero had also emerged in Major Sonam Wangchoo, who was awarded Mahavir Chakra. In the year 2008, I had privilege of meeting him at a program of Delhi Metro and NCC.

Captain Singh had showed us all the famous war-time posts like Tololing Top, Batra Top, Sando Top, Rocky Nob, Three Pimples, Rhino Horns, 5140, 4875 Tops, etc which remained in limelight on news channels during Kargil War. By this time, we were feeling physically tired but mentally we were highly satisfied as this was the most fascinating day of our life when we could see such wonderful places. When we reached Army Guest House, the proud memories of brave soldiers kept revisiting our minds.

Next day in the morning, we went to see Complex 43. This complex is situated on LOC, from where Pakistani soldiers can be seen manning their posts. While I was observing and taking photographs of the surroundings, some Pakistani soldiers came out to see us. Soldiers posted there informed us that prior to 1971, this

A Beautiful View of Dras Valley

Author along with a friend Gaurav Pathak and the army man Limbu at Sando Top

area was under the control of Pakistan and for sending any truck to Leh, their permission was required as main road used to pass through here only. After 1971, all such restrictions have been cleared. There near this post, one Board was placed indicating that POK (Pak Occupied Kashmir) is 600 metres away. I, like all other Indians, sincerely wish that one day entire Kashmir will be under our control after acquiring the land that rightfully belongs to India.

Weather was very good and clear visibility enabled us to see up to a great distance. Therefore, we could easily spot Pakistani post with their flag fluttering atop. All this would remain etched in our memories for the lifetime. We returned to Army's Mess with the rich collection of proud and patriotic moments in our hearts.

After having lunch, we thanked our gracious hosts and with heavy heart bade farewell to Kargil and proceeded for Amarnath. After travelling for some time, Zojila Pass arrived.

Zojila is the same place beyond which Indian Army had used tanks as a surprising move during 1947 Kashmir War. This strategic masterstroke had shocked the Pakistanis as they could not have imagined this in the wildest of their dreams. In the 1999 War, 527 soldiers had become martyrs and other 1,363 were injured.

Whenever you get an opportunity to visit these places please avail it to pay your homage and gratitude to these great martyrs. □

11
REFERENCES

Documentaries

- Guns and Glory Series: India's Wars by Headlines Today.
- Pradhan Mantri Series: ABP News (Presented by Shekhar Kapoor).
- Chander Shekhar Azad, documentary by Ministry of Information & Broadcasting.
- History of Cellular Jail – *Kala Pani*, documentary by Ministry of Information & Broadcasting.
- Sh. Bhagat Singh – The Story of the Legend. Documentary by Livehimmatpura.
- Shaheed Bhagat Singh/Documentary/Navalpreet Rangi.
- Madan Lal Dhingra, documentary by Darshan Lal Jain.
- A Tribute to Shaheed Bhagat Singh – The Ever-Loved National Hero by Ministry of Information & Broadcasting.
- PM Modi visits National Martyrs' Memorial at Hussainiwala village in Firozpur, Punjab – Narendra Modi Channel.
- "Param Veer Chakra" – a serial made by Chetan Anand and telecast on Doordarshan.
- Films made on Bhagat Singh.

Information/Details collected from the following Museums/Memorials:

- Bhartiya Vayu Sena Sangrahalaya (Indian Air Force Museum), Palam Road, Near Hanuman Mandir, Palam, New Delhi.
- Rashtriya Abhilekhagar Sangrahalaya, Janpath Road, New Delhi.
- Nehru Smarak Sangrahalaya, Teen Murti Bhawan, New Delhi.
- Indira Gandhi Smarak Sangrahalaya, 1, Safadarjung Road, New Delhi.
- Sainya Vidroh Smarak, Near Hindu Rao Hospital and Adarsh Nagar, Metro Station, New Delhi.
- Nicholson Kabragaah, Club Road, Civil Lines, New Delhi.
- Information from Bhagat Singh, Rajguru and Veer Savarkar Sangrahalaya.
- Rajkiya Swatantrata Sangram Sangrahalaya, Meerut, Uttar Pradesh.
- Swatantrata Sangram Sangrahalaya, Lal Qila, Delhi.
- Swatantrata Senani Sangrahalaya, Lal Qila, Delhi.
- Bhartiya Yuddha Smarak Sangrahalaya, Lal Qila, Delhi.
- Mumtaz Mahal Sangrahalaya.
- Mutiny Memorial, Kashmere Gate, Delhi.
- Birthplace and Museum of Chandrashekhar Azad, Chandrashekhar Azad Nagar, Madhya Pradesh.

Books

- *Shreshtha Sainik Kahania – Lt. Genl. Yashwant* Mande – Prabhat Prakashan, New Delhi.
- *Mai Bhagat Singh Bol Raha Hun* – Sankalankarta Anil Kumar, Pratibha Pratisthan, New Delhi.
- *Sansmitiaya* – Shiv Verma, National Book Trust of India.
- *Param Veer Vijeta* – Balbir Saxena – Mansi Prakashan, New Delhi.
- *Bhartiya Sena Ke Shurveer* – Maj. Gen. Shubhi Sood – Prabhat Prakashan, New Delhi.

- *Mahakrantikari Mangal Pandey* – Dinkar Kumar – Children's Book Temple, Delhi.
- *Netaji Subhash: Chitramayi Jeewani* – Rajendra Patoria – Vidya Vihar, New Delhi.
- *Amar Balidaani Tatya Tope* – Mahesh Sharma, Prabhat Paper Backs – enterprise of Prabhat Prakashan, New Delhi.
- *Amar Shaheed Sardar Bhagat Singh* – Jitendra Nath Sanyal – National Book Trust of India.
- *1857: Itihas Aur Sanskritee* – Editor Murali Manohar Prasad Singh, Rekha Awasthi – Prakashan Vibhag, Soochna evam Prasaran Mantralaya, Govt. of India.
- *Attarah sau Sattavan ka Swantrata Sangram* – Surendranath Sen – Prakashan Vibhag, Soochna and Prasaran Mantralaya, Govt. of India.
- *Shaura Tejo* – Jaswant Singh and Gen Suraj Bhatia – Prabhat Prakashan, New Delhi.
- *Rang De Basanti Chola* – Bhishma Sahni, Kitab Ghar Prakashan, New Delhi.
- *Kala Pani* – Vinayak Damodar Das Savarkar— Prabhat Prakashan, New Delhi.
- *Ek Sena Dhakshya Ki Aatma Katha* – Gen. J.J. Singh, Prabhat Prakashan, New Delhi.
- *1962 The War That Wasn't* (e-book) – Shiv Kunal Verma – Alpesh Book Company.
- *Bhagat Singh's "Jail Note Book"*: Malvinder Jeet Singh Warraich & Harish Jain – Unistar Books Pvt. Ltd.
- *Bhagat Singh: The Eternal Rebel* – Malvinder Jeet Singh Warraich, Publication: Unistar Books Pvt. Ltd.
- *A Revolutionary History of Inter-war India* – Kama Maclean Publisher: Penguin Books.

□

12
LIST OF PARAM VEER CHAKRA AWARDES

Rank	Name	Regiment	Date	Place
Major	# Somnath Sharma	Kumaun Regiment	3/11/1947	Badgam J&K
Nayak	# Yadunath Singh	Rajput Regiment	6/2/1948	Naushera J&K
2nd Lt.	Rama Raghoba Rane	Engineering wing	8/4/1948	Do
Co. Haval. Maj.	# Piru Singh Shekhawat	Rajputana Rifles	17/7/1948	Tithwal, J&K
Lance Nayak	Karam Singh	Indian Army	13/10/1948	Do
Capt.	# Gur bachan Singh	Gorkha Rifles	5/12/1961	Elizabeth ville Kango
Maj.	Dhan Singh Thapa	Do	20/10 1962	Laddakh, J&K
Subedar	# Joginder Singh	Sikh Regimen	23/10/1962	Tongpen La NEFA
Maj.	# Shaitan Singh	Kumaun Regiment	18/10/1962	Rejang La J&K
Com Qtr. Master	# Abdul Hamid	The Grenadiers	10/9/1965	Khemkaran Sector
Lt. Col.	Ardesir Burzorji	India Army	15/10/1965	Fillor Sector Pak
Lance Nayak	# Albert Ekka	Brigade of Di Guards	3/12/1971	Ganga Sagar Aga
Flying Officer	# Nirmal Jeet Sekhow	Indian Army	14/12/1971	Srinagar

2nd Lt.	# Arun Khetrapal	Do	16/12/1971	Barpind
Major	Hoshiyar Singh	The Granadiers	17/12/1971	Basantar River
Nayab Subedar	Bana Singh	J&K Light Infantry	23/5/1987	Siachen
Major	# Ramaswami Parmeshwaran	Mahar Regiment	25/11/1987	Sri Lanka
Capt.	# Manoj Kr. Pandey	Gorkha Rifles	3/7/1999	Khaiubar
Grenediar	Yogendra Singh Yadav	The Grenediers	4/7/1999	Tiger Hill
Rifle Man	Sanjay Kumar	J&K Rifles	5/7/1999	Area Flat Top
Capt.	# Vikram Batra	Do	6/7/1999	Point 5140, 4875

 # Posthumously

1857			
Place	**State**	**Nearest Railway Stn/Airport**	**Distance from Delhi**
Barrackpore	West Bengal	Howrah	1465 km
Jhansi	UP	Jhansi	464 km
Meerut	UP	Meerut City	70 km
Bithur	UP	Kanpur Central	499 km
Kali Paltan Mandir, Meerut	UP	Meerut City	70 km
Pune	Maharashtra	Pune	1464 km
Yevla	Do	Yevla/Manmad	1232 km
Bhagur	Do	Nasik	1288 km
Gwalior	MP	Gwalior	350 km
Kranti Teerth Mandvi	Gujarat	Gandi Dham/Bhuj	1209 km
Vellore	Tamil Nadu	Vellore	2208 km
Mutiny Memorial and Ajitgarh Memorial	New Delhi	Delhi	0

Lal Qila	Do	Delhi	0

Hussainiwala, Firozpur			
Shahidee Smarak, Hussainiwala Border	Punjab	Firozpur	431 kms
Khatkal Kala	Punjab	Ludhiana/Fillor	329 kms
Wagah Border	Punjab	Amritsar	483 kms
Birthplace of Sukhdev Thapar	Chouda Bazar	Ludhiana	323 kms
Kot Lakhpat	Rann, Kutch	Gujarat Bhuj	1292 kms
Leh	J&K	Leh Airport	1292 kms
Museum Rajguru Nagar	Maharastra	Pune/Kher	1389 kms
Chandra Shekhar Azad Nagar	MP	Dahod (Gujarat)	875 kms
Chandra Shekhar Park	UP	Allahabad	687 kms
Netaji Bhawan	W Bengal	Howrah	1463 kms

Kala Pani, Cellular Jail			
Cellular Jail	Andman Nicobar Island	Port Blair Airport	2493 kms
Veer Savarkar Smarak	Mumbai	Mumbai	1413 kms
Birthplace of Veer Savarkar	Bhagur	Nasik	1278 kms

Jallianwala Bag and Wagah Border			
Jallianwala Bagh	Punjab	Amritsar	447 kms
Swarna Mandir	Do	Do	448 kms
Wagah Border	Do	Do	483 kms
Durgiana Mandir	Do	Do	449 kms
Attari	Do	Do	475 kms

INDO-PAK War, 1947			
Zojila Pass	J&K	Srinagar	937 kms
Srinagar	Do	Do	838 kms
Baltaal	Do	Do	928 kms
Kargil	Do	Do	1037 kms
Dras	Do	Do	976 kms
Sonmarg	Do	Do	914 kms
Naushera Area	Do	Jammu	692 kms
Badgaam Area	Do	Srinagar	841 kms
Mohd. Usman ji ki Mazar	New Delhi	New Delhi	0

Indo-China War, 1962			
Shaheed Smarak Chushul	Leh, J&K	Leh/Kusok Airport	1057 kms
Nathu La	Sikkim	New Jalpai Gudi	1652 kms
Sela Pass	Arunanchal Pradesh	Guwahati	2267 kms
Boom La	Tawang, Arunanchal	Guwahati	2421 kms
Jaswant Singh Rawat War Memorial	Tawang, Arunanchal	Guwahati	2421 kms

Indo-Pak War, 1965			
Abdul Hameed ji ki Mazar	Punjab	Khemkaran/ Amritsar	450 kms

Indo-Pak War, 1971			
Longewala and Tanot Mata Mandir	Rajasthan	Jaisalmer	825 kms
Diu	Daman & Diu	Somnath/Veraval	362 kms
Bhartiya Vayu Sena Museum and War Memorial	Palam, New Delhi	New Delhi	0

Indo-Pak War, 1999			
Kargil Sector	J&K	Srinagar	1037 kms
Dras Sector	Do	Do	976 kms
Batalik Sector	Do	Do	976 kms
Srinagar	Do	Do	838 kms
Siachen	Do	Do	1455 kms
Mashkoh Valley	Do	Do	1001 kms
Dras War Memorial	Do	Do	976 kms
Zojila Darra	Do	Do	937 kms
Kala Pahar Chowki	Do	Do	1057 kms
Tiger Hill	Do	Do	976 kms
Vijayant Thapar Smarak	NOIDA, UP	Botanical Garden Metro Station	18 kms

□

13
LIST OF WAR MEMORIALS IN INDIA

Punjab	
Place/At	**Name of War Memorial**
Adampur, Punjab (Air Force Station)	Air Force Station, Aadmpur, Vayu Shakti Sthal
Amritsar, Punjab (Military Station Khasa)	Dograi War Memorial
Amritsar, Punjab (Near Ratoke Gurudwara)	5 Gorkha Rifles War Memorial
Amritsar, Punjab (Pulkanzari, Dhanaya Kalan)	Pulkanzari War Memorial
Asal Uttar, Punjab (Taran-Taran Saheb)	C.Q.M.H. Abdul Hameed P.V.C. Memorial
Asal Uttar, Punjab (Taran Taran Sahib, Khemkaran Valtoha Road)	7 Granediers War Memorial
Bhatinda, Punjab (Airport Station, Bhisiyana)	Sq. Leader Ajai Ahuja Memorial
Bhura Kuhna, Taran-Taran District, Punjab	2/Lt. J.P. Gaur Memorial
Bhura Kuhna, Taran-Taran District.	2-Madras Memorial
Bhura Kuhna, Punjab (Bhikhiwind-Khemkaran Road)	Sappar Harak Singh Memorial
Chandigarh	Chandigarh Yuddha Smritee
Fazilka, Punjab (Village Asafwala)	Aasadwala, 1971 War Memorial
Firozpur Cantt, Punjab	Sahazara, 1971 Memorial
Firozpur, Punjab	Burki, 1964 Memorial
Firozpur, Punjab	Saragadhi Memorial

Firozpur (Golden Arrow House Crossing)	Sutlej Campaign War Memorial
Firozpur, Punjab (Village Mahadipur)	Mahar War Memorial
Firozpur, Punjab (Golden Arrow House Crossing)	VI K.E.O. Cavellery War Memorial
Firozpur, Punjab (Do)	Brownlos Punjabi, War Memorial
Firozpur, Punjab (Do)	19,22 x 24 Punjabi War Memorial 1914-19
Firozpur, Punjab (Near Mehandipur Village, close to Peer Baba Mazar)	Sq. Ldr Raman Uppal Memorial
Firozpur, Punjab (Cantt. Gen.Hospital, Family Wing)	Gallipoli Memorial Tablet
Gurdaspur, Punjab (Batala)	Batala War Memorial
Gurudaspur, Punjab (Dera Baba Nanak)	Dera Baba Nanak, 1971 Memorial
Halwara, Punjab (Air Force Station)	Air Force Station, Halwara War Memorial
Hussainiwala, Firozpur	Rashtriya Shaheed Smarak, Hussainiwala
Kapurthala, Punjab	Lt. Jhaggar Singh War Memorial (WW-1)
Kapurthal Punjab (Near Station HQ)	Imperial State Forces War Memorial (WW-1)
Pathankot, Punjab (Air Force Station)	Wall of Silence
Patiala, Punjab (Stadium Road)	Patiala State Forces Memorial
Patiala, Punjab (Y.P.S. Chowk)	Black Eliphant Division Memorial

Jammu-Kashmir	
Baramullah	1, Sikh War Memorial
Baramullah	Daggar Memorial
Dras, Kargil (Bimbat)	Bimbat, 8 Division Kargil War Memorial
Jammu (Air Force Station)	Kodors War Memorial
Jammu (Bahu Vali Rakh)	Balidaan Stambha

Jammu (Near Tiger Parkcent Mary Public School)	Tiger War Memorial
Leh	Leh (1962, 1965, 1971) War Memorial
Leh	Leh (1947-48) War Memorial
Maachal	Sahi Memorial Hospital
Punch	Lok Bahadur Stadium Memorial
Rajouri	Hall of Fame
Sambha	3, Madras Memorial
Sambha (Mortuary)	2/Lt. Arun Khetrapal PVC War Memorial
Sambha (N.H.1)	Major R.S. Rajwat Memorial
Satwari Cantonment (opp: C.S.D. Canteen)	Jammu-Kashmir State Forces War Memorial
Siachen	Siachen War Memorial
Rejang La	Rejang La War Memorial
Srinagar	15 Core War Memorials
Udhampur	Dhurva Shaheed Smarak
B.B. Cantonment, Srinagar	O.P. Rakshak Memorial
Chushul	Chushul War Memorial

Uttar Pradesh	
Agra (Para Brigade)	Shatrujeet War Memorial
Allahabad (Old Cantt)	4, Infantry Division War Memorial
Allahabad (Bamrauli)	Indian Air Force Central Air Command War Memorial
Bareilly (Jat Regimental Centre)	Jat Memorial War Memorial
Faizabad	C.M.P. x 7 Infantry Brigade War Memorial
Faizabad (Dogra Regimental Centre)	Dogra War Memorial
Faizabad (HQ, Madhya Uttar)	H.Q. 7 Infantry Brigade War Memorial
Farrukhabad (Sikh LI Regimental Centre)	Sikh Light Infantry War Memorial

Fatehgarh (Rajput Regimental Centre)	Rajput Regiment War Memorial
Gorakhpur (Air Force Station)	Air Force Station War Memorial
Jhansi Cantt.	White Tiger War Memorial
Kunraghat, Gorakhpur (Gorkha Recruiting Centre)	Gorkha Brigade War Memorial
Lucknow (A.M.C. Centre and College)	Armed Forces Medical Services War Memorial
Lucknow (Mahatma Gandhi Road)	Smriti ka War Memorial
Lucknow (11 G.R. Regimental Centre)	11, Gorkha Rifles War Memorial
Mathura (HQ 1 Core Complex)	1, Core War Memorial
Meerut Cantt.	Pyne Division War Memorial
Meerut Cantt.	Saragarhi Memorial
NOIDA (Near Army Public School)	Noida Shaheed Smarak
Sarsawa, Saharanpur	Air Force Station, Sarsawa War Memorial
Varanasi (39, Gorkha Training Centre)	39 Gorkha Training Centre War Memorial

Rajasthan	
Alwar (Company Garden)	Alwar War Memorial
Churu (Distt. HQ, Sector 2)	Shaheed Smarak Memorial
Jaipur	Sadhewala War Memorial
Jaipur (M.I. Road)	Shaheed Smarak War Memorial
Jaipur (Rajpath Road)	Amar Jawan Jyoti War Memorial
Jaisalmer (Air Force Station)	Vijay Stambh, Vijay Smarak
Jodhpur (Beyond Ummed Bhawan Palace)	Konark War Memorial
Jodhpur (Paota Circle)	Major Shaitan Singh PVC Memorial
Longewala Sector	War Memorial BP
Longewala	168, F.D. Regiment War Memorial
Sri Ganga Nagar (Karanpur Town)	Nagi War Memorial

New Delhi	
New Delhi (Teen Murti Marg)	Teen Murti Memorial
New Delhi (Rajpath)	India Gate
New Delhi (Rajputana Rifles, Regt. Centre)	Rajputana Rifles War Memorial
New Delhi (Near Air Force Museum Palam)	Air Force Station, Palam War Memorial

Karnataka	
Bengaluru (Along Central Parade Ground)	Madras Sappers War Memorial
Bengaluru (A.S.C. Centre and College)	Army Service Core War Memorial
Bengaluru (A.S.C. Centre and College)	Army Transport Animals Memorial
Bengaluru (C.M.P. Centre)	Core of Military Police War Memo.
Bengaluru (at the end of Brigade Road)	Pioneer Core War Memorial
Bengaluru (H.Q. Training Command)	Indian Air Force Trg. Command Memo.
Bengaluru (M.E.G. and Centre)	British War Memorial
Bengaluru (Parashoot Reg. Centre)	Parashoot Regt. War Memorial
Belgaum (Maratha Light Inf. Centre)	Maratha Light Infantry War Memorial
Beedar (Air Force Station)	Air Force Station, Beedar Memorial
Anjadeev Ireland	Anjadeev Ireland, War Memorial

Gujarat	
Ahmedabad Cantt.	Golden Katar War Memorial
Ahmedabad (Near Shahibag State Guest House)	Ahmedabad War Memorial
Bhuj (Rajaram Park)	Bhuj War Memorial
Gandhi Nagar (Chiloda Military Centre)	Parvat Ali War Memorial

Jamnagar (Air Force Station)	Vijay Stambh
Jamnagar (Rozy Ireland)	I.N.S. Valsura War Memorial
Jamnagar (Air Force Station)	Jamnagar War Memorial

Madhya Pradesh	
Bhopal (3 EME Centre)	No. 3 EME Centre War Memorial
Bhopal (Core HQ)	Sudarshan Chakra War Memorial
Jabalpur (1 Military Traning Regiment)	Core of Signals War Memorial
Jabalpur (Grenadiers Regiment Center)	The Grenadiers War Memorial
Jabalpur (Jammu and Kashmir Rifles Regiment Centre)	J&K Rifles War Memorial
Jabalpur (C.M.M. School)	Kangla Togbi War Memorial
Mhow	Infantry Memorial
Saugor	Shahbaz War Memorial

Haryana	
Ambala (Air Force Station)	Air Force Station, Ambala Frozen Tears Memorial
Chandi Mandir Cantt.	Veer Smritee Western Command War Memorial
Gurgaon (John Hall)	Gurgaon Shaheed Sthal
Hissar (MD University)	Amar Jawan War Memorial
Jhajjar (Sainik Rest House)	Jhajjar War nemorial
Jind (Distt. Court)	Jind War Memorial
Narwana (Navdeep Stadium)	Narwana War Memorial
Bahadurgarh	Bahadurgarh War Memorial
Rohtak (Mansa Sarovar)	Yuddaha Shaheed Smarak

Arunachal Pradesh	
Arunachal Pradesh (18 kms. from Valong)	Helmet Top War Memorial
Manmao Post	Manmao War Memorial
Nura Nang (25 kms. from Tawang)	Jaswantgarh War Memorial
Tawang	Tawang War Memorial

Valong	Valong War Memorial
Valong	Hut of Remembrance
Valong	Air Force Memorial, Valong

Jharkhand	
Ramgarh Cantt. (Sikh Regimental Centre)	Saragarhi War Memorial
Ramgarh Cantt. (Sikh Regimental Centre)	Sikh Regimental War Centre
Ramgarh Cantt. (Punjab Regimental Centre)	Punjab Regiment War Memorial
Ranchi (Dipatoli Cantt.)	Jharkhand War Memorial

Andhra Pradesh	
Dundigal (Air Force Academy)	Air Force Academy Flight Crew Memorial
Hyderabad (Mehdipattanam)	Basantar War Memorial
Secunderabad Cantt. (1, EME Centre)	1, EME Centre War Memorial
Secunderabad (A.O.C. Centre)	A.O.C. Centre War Memorial
Secunderabad (Army Training Ground)	Virula Saini's Smarak
Secunderabad (Bovenpalli)	Mighty Bombardiers War Memorial
Vishakahapattanam (Ramkrishna Beach)	Victory at Sea War Memorial

Meghalaya	
Shillong (58, Gorkha Training Centre)	58, Gorkha Training Centre War Memorial
Shillong (Happy Valley)	Assam Regiment War Memorial
Shillong	1971 War Memorial

West Bengal	
Binnaguri (Binnaguri Military Station)	Bogra War Memorial
Darjeeling	Batasia War Memorial

Hansimara, Jalpaiguri (Air Force Station)	Air Force Station, Hansimara War Memorial
Howrah (on the bank of Hooghly River)	Laskar War Memorial
Kolkatta (Red Road)	The Glorious Dead War Memorial
Kolkatta (College Square)	49, Bengali War Memorial
Kolkatta (Fort William)	Eastern Command Vijay Smarak
Sukna Military Station (Near Siliguri)	33, Core Vijay Smarak War Memorial

Uttarakhand	
Dehradun (Indian Military Academy)	Indian Military Academy War Memorial
Dehradun (Lal Gate)	Lal Gate War Memorial
Lancedown (Garhwal Rifles Regimental Centre)	Garhwal Rifles War Memorial
Pithoragarh	Maharaj ke Memorial Park
Ranikhet (Kumaun Reg. Centre)	Kumaun Regiment War Memorial
Rurki (Rudkee)	Bengal Sappers War Memorial

Himachal Pradesh	
Dharamshala	Dharamshala Shaheed Smarak
Jutogh Cantonment, Simla	3, Mountain Artillery Brigade War Memorial
Subathu (14, G.T.C.)	14, G.T.C. War Memorial

Assam	
Dibrugarh	D.A.H. War Memorial
Guwahati (Air Force Station)	Air Force Station, Guwahati War Memorial
Mohanbari (Air Force Station)	Air Force Station, Mohanbari War Memories
Silchar (Kheba Hills)	Amar Jawan War Memorial
Tejpur (Air Force Station)	Air Force Station, Tejpur War Memorial
Tejpur (HQ 4, Core)	4, Core War Memorial

Tamil Nadu	
Aavdi, Chennai (in front of Depot House)	Air Force Station, Avadi War Memorial
Tiruchirapalli (Gandhi Market)	Tiruchirapalli WW-1 Memorial
Wellington (Madras Regimental Centre)	Madras Regiment War Memorial

Kerala	
Kannennor Distt. (Defence Security Core Centre)	Defence Security Core, Gaurav Sthal
Ejhimala (Indian Naval Academy)	Indian Naval Academy Ejhimala War Me
Kocchi (Naval Base Kocchi)	I.N.S. Vendurthi War Memorial
Thiruvananthapuram	The Bogra Memorial Hut

Tripura	
Agartala	Agartala War Memorial

Bihar	
Danapur (Bihar Regimental Centre)	Bihar Regiment War Memorial

Diu	
Diu (Anti-Submarine Warfare School)	I.N.S. Khukhree Memorial

Manipur	
Imphal (Village Khejang)	Kangla Togbi War Memorial
Lemakhodag	Shantivan War Memorial

Nagaland	
Jakhama Military Station	Orchid Memorial

Source: List available on the website of Foreign Ministry (Govt. of India).

□□□